A Very British Genre

A Short History of
British Fantasy and Science Fiction

Paul Kincaid

BRITISH SCIENCE FICTION ASSOCIATION
1995

A Very British Genre

First published in Great Britain 1995
by The British Science Fiction Association Limited
60 Bournemouth Road, Folkestone, Kent CT19 5AZ

ISBN: 1-870824-37-7

Printed by:

M & T Kelleher
8 Winchelsea Road
London E7 0AG

Contents

Acknowledgements

THIS HISTORY OF British Science Fiction and Fantasy is the view of one person, and as partial and idiosyncratic as that suggests. But it couldn't have been written without a lot of help and support from other people. I am more grateful than I can adequately express to Paul Allwood, K.V. Bailey, Elizabeth Billinger, John Clute, Dave Langford, Andy Sawyer and Chris Terran, whose comments and suggestions helped me avoid some of the worst errors I might otherwise have been guilty of. I want to thank Mark Plummer and Roger Robinson, without whose help this history would probably never have seen the light of day. I particularly want to single out my wife, Maureen Kincaid Speller, who laboured over the manuscript to make it better than it might have been by my efforts alone.

I would also like to thank Colin Greenland who, unknowingly, provided me with two of my chapter titles and Dave Hicks who provided artwork for a BSFA poster which I have appropriated for the cover of this book.

This publication was put together with the enthusiastic support of the British Science Fiction Association, and I want to thank all the committee.

The BSFA occupies a very important place not just in British science fiction but in the whole world of sf. It is an organisation which brings together authors, publishers, critics booksellers, fans and readers, it provides a vital forum for everyone involved in or who derives enjoyment from science fiction. The BSFA doesn't just deserve your support, it also offers a great deal to everyone, from its magazines, its services for writers, its Information Service and more. To join the BSFA, or if you want more information, you should write to: Alison Cook, Membership Secretary, 52 Woodhill Drive, Grove, Nr Wantage, Oxon OX12 0DF

This publication was made possible thanks to money donated to the BSFA by Sou'Wester, the 1994 British Easter convention.

Introduction

SCIENCE FICTION IS not a distinctly British genre. Though Mary Shelley and H.G. Wells, among others, can be claimed to be the founders of the genre, others might make a similar claim for French writers (Verne) and American (Poe). Since the 1920s the principal home of science fiction seems to have been America, though the genre has become increasingly international with prominent writers coming from as far afield as Australia, Japan and Poland. Much the same is true of genre fantasy. Nevertheless, fantastic literature in Britain does seem to have developed a characteristic tone and style, it has given rise to some of the significant innovators in the genre, from J.R.R. Tolkien to J.G. Ballard, and it remains a leading voice in science fiction and fantasy throughout the world.

What it is that makes British science fiction and fantasy distinctive is not so easy to say. Books and articles galore have already been written on the subject, doubtless more will follow, but no readily accepted conclusions have been reached.

In discussing the history of the genre in Britain I don't want to suggest that separate development is somehow behind it all. Cross-fertilisation has been a constant feature of science fiction, and British sf writers picked up on the American innovations of cyberpunk, for instance, as readily as American writers picked up on the New Wave. Still, a history should help to show how British science fiction has become what it is and so offer a perspective on those distinguishing features. After all, if we are to accept Brian Aldiss's claim that the publication of *Frankenstein* marked the birth of science fiction, then we are talking about a genre that is fast approaching its bicentennial and which, to judge from the proliferation of new British writers, is healthier than it has ever been before.

In what follows, therefore, I am taking an openly partisan approach to science fiction and fantasy. I will trace the genre from its origins with Wells and Shelley and before, through scientific romance and cosy catastrophe to the new wave and up to new writers like Jeff Noon, Michael Marshall Smith and Alison Sinclair who have seen their first novels appear in the mid-1990s. Along the route I will try to distinguish some thread that is typically British, that marks British fantastic literature out as a viable, flourishing and fascinating branch of the genre in its own right.

Any work of this type is bound to be partial. In particular, I could not hope to do justice to the breadth and variety of British writing in science fiction, fantasy, the ghost story or horror in anything less than a full and probably very densely packed book. Inevitably, therefore, I have had to make decisions as I went along about what to include and what to omit. As a result, there are writers, from J.D. Beresford to D.G. Compton, Michael Scott Rohan and John Whitbourn, who are not mentioned here who could be included in anyone else's list of key British writers, while others receive only a passing mention. Any other historian might have included these but excluded others I have mentioned, such are the exigencies of a work of this nature.

The essay concludes with a chronology and a checklist of contemporary British writers of science fiction and fantasy. I hope this will act not just as a reminder of how lively and varied British sf is at the moment, but also as an introduction to writers who are all making a significant contribution to our genre.

Chapter One

The Monster Wakes

WHERE DO THE origins of science fiction lie?

People have been telling stories as long as they have had language, and mostly those stories have been fantastic. Stories of gods who dwell in the rocks or rivers, sprites who emerge from trees or caves, monsters who wait beyond the horizon, heroes who battle and win; they form the basis of our religions and our mythologies. Inevitably, when men and women stopped telling tales around the campfire and started writing them down, the first works of literature to emerge were fantastic. *The Epic of Gilgamesh* in the Middle East, *The Iliad* and *The Odyssey* in Greece, *Beowulf* here in Britain, all echoed the pattern and content of centuries if not millenia of pre-literate story-telling.

These stories still provide a framework around which much of modern literature is shaped. Sometimes this may be overtly fantastic, as in Geoff Ryman's use of *Gilgamesh* in *The Warrior Who Carried Life* (1985) or John Gardner's retelling of *Beowulf* in *Grendel* (1971), sometimes not, as when James Joyce appropriated the format of Homer's *Odyssey* for his own *Ulysses* (1922). It is not surprising, therefore, that mythic stories such as these should provide the key to most of our literary history. As prose began to emerge, first alongside epic verse then superseding it as a popular literary medium, it made use of the same elements of gods, monsters and heroes.

The first significant work of prose fiction in Britain was *Le Morte d'Arthur* (1485) by Sir Thomas Malory. King Arthur had long been a staple of the English romantic imagination. He had appeared in pre-Norman chronicles and early-Norman pseudo-histories, such as the chronicles of Nennius and the outrageously fantastical *History of the Kings of Britain* (c. 1138) by Geoffrey of Monmouth, while the anonymous poem *Sir Gawain and the Green Knight* (14th cent.) was one of the first acknowledged masterpieces of English literature. He had been claimed as ancestor by several kings, was the proclaimed inspiration for chivalric orders such as the Order of the Garter founded by Edward III, had loaned his name to various ill-fated princes who never seemed to reach the throne, and was even behind one of the great medieval public relations coups when his grave was "discovered" at Glastonbury. Even in Europe his exploits had been celebrated in troubadour ballads and the stories of writers such as Chrétien de Troyes and Wolfram von Eschenbach. But Malory brought these tales together and gave them a (more or less) coherent form. The result was a work replete with magic:

A Very British Genre

Merlin and the Fisher King, Excalibur and the Grail, Morgan le Fay and the Isle of Avalon. A curious combination of Celtic and Norman influences, rich with both Christian and pre-Christian imagery, and full enough of archetypes to keep any psychiatrist happy, the stories of Arthur and his circle, collectively known as the Matter of Britain, have had an indelible effect on the literary imagination of the entire English-speaking world. From the poems of Tennyson's *Idylls of the King* (1891) to Lerner and Lowe's musical *Camelot* (1960) they have provided the acceptable, popular face of fantasy. More than that, the stories have been endlessly mined for symbols and plots by writers, in and out of the genre, as varied as Iris Murdoch, Anthony Powell, Alan Garner, Robert Nye, Samuel R. Delany and Poul Anderson. Here, if anywhere, lies the origin of British fantasy.

But it would be wrong to claim just one parent for a literature as protean as fantasy and science fiction. If the Matter of Britain provided a source of inspiration, there were other writers who contributed to the diversity of our literary heritage. Until the eighteenth century, fantasy and fiction were virtually synonymous; even when realism began to emerge strongly as a literary form during the eighteenth century it was seen as just one mode among others, no more nor less important than fantasy, satire, the picaresque. However, during the second half of the 19th century, rhetoric began to be replaced in universities with the study of a canonical list of great books. In America this list was set by the Harvard canon, in Britain it owes much to the work of academic critics such as F.R. Leavis in the early years of this century. The list of key books, particularly where it encompassed contemporary or near-contemporary writers, was predominantly realist in tone. This canonisation of literature, associated as it was with the Victorian tradition of *belle-lettres*, introduced notions of high and low culture, with realism elevated to the high ranks and fantasy relegated to the low. Before this distinction set in, from the sixteenth century until the end of the nineteenth century, writers were as likely to produce works of fantasy as any other mode. Spenser transformed the court of Elizabeth into a realm of faerie in *The Faerie Queen* (1590-96). Shakespeare wrote fantasies such as *A Midsummer Night's Dream* (1596) and *The Tempest* (1611) alongside histories, satires, love stories and more.

Writing in Latin while serving as an envoy in Flanders, Sir Thomas More wrote a satire on his country so savage that Karl Marx would quote it nearly four hundred years later. It would give a new word to the language and would later bear fruit as one of the most distinctive forms of science fiction, *Utopia* (1516). Couched as an extraordinary traveller's tale, it presented an idealised portrait of how much better things might be if only human values were different. More was writing at the beginning of a two-hundred-year period which saw terrible religious and political upheavals in Britain. Henry VIII's break with Rome launched religious persecutions, burnings at the stake, the suppression at various times of Catholics and Protestants, the rise of puritanism, Civil War, regicide, the Bloody Assizes and the Glorious Revolution. Amid this chaos, people were forced to find their own way to live, and so the period saw the flight to new worlds of promise by groups such as the Pilgrim Fathers and the creation of utopian communities such as Gerrard Winstanley's Diggers. All of this, particularly in the century from 1600, was accompanied by More's literary heritage: an incredible flowering of utopian stories and marvellous journeys presenting imaginative ways to escape the horrors of daily life, the most notable of which was *The New Atlantis* (1627) by Francis Bacon. Some were undoubtedly suppressed as too subversive while others became more and more fanciful. Daniel Defoe, who would write a classic novel of escape and establish a whole category of sf (the "robinsonade") with his most famous work, *Robinson Crusoe* (1719), also worked within one of the most popular and most fantastical of these satirical utopian modes, the trip to the Moon, with *The Consolidator or Memoirs of Sundry*

A Short History of British Fantasy and Science Fiction

Transactions from the World in the Moon (1705), though the best and most lasting of these satires was undoubtedly Jonathan Swift's *Gulliver's Travels* (1726). It is interesting to note that among the targets of Swift's attack were the men of learning, the scientists of their day. Charles II had created the Royal Society, John Locke had propounded the empiricism which would become the scientific method we know today, William Harvey had discovered the circulation of blood, Flamsteed was investigating the stars, Newton was studying gravity and optics. Political turmoil had given way to intellectual ferment. This was the Age of Reason, of lone polymaths conducting in back rooms whatever experiments took their fancy, the originals of science fiction's mad scientists. The discoveries they made, the inventions they created, were part of the intellectual currency of the age – and the effects were starting to find their way into the satires and marvellous journeys of literature. The machine that took Defoe's protagonist to the Moon, the flying machine that featured in Samuel Johnson's *Rasselas* (1759): ur-science fiction was beginning its transformation into the literature we recognise today.

At this time a further change in the social and the imaginative shape of British society was happening that would complete the transformation. From the middle of the seventeenth century, gathering pace particularly during the eighteenth century, the Industrial Revolution was changing the country forever. Industry developed rapidly and the countryside was enclosed, with a consequent drift of rural workers into the growing cities. First canals then railways sliced through the landscape to provide faster and yet faster means of transport. The Age of Reason, with the rise of science, had created machines, from the Spinning Jenny to the steam engine, whose effects could never have been imagined. Nor did this increasing mechanisation happen in isolation. A powerful new elite of wealthy industrialists emerged, a series of Reform Bills throughout the nineteenth century undermined the old order, an underclass of wage slaves and urban poor was created for the first time ever. And a new way of looking at the world emerged from the Palladian mansions and landscaped gardens of the new leisured class.

The Romantic imagination gave particular prominence to nature. In a realm where even the countryside was being tamed by landscape gardeners, wild places and unruly storms were held to contain great truths, to hint at the sublime. Coupled with a morbid fascination for ruins (the late eighteenth century saw a popular fascination with archaeology fuelled by Napoleon's discoveries in Egypt and expressed best in Percy Bysshe Shelley's poem "Ozymandias" (1818)) this romanticism gave birth to the Gothic. In highly popular novels such as *The Castle of Otranto* (1765) by Horace Walpole, *Vathek* (1786) by William Beckford, *The Mysteries of Udolpho* (1794) by Ann Radcliffe and *The Monk* (1796) by Matthew Lewis the dark stuff of dreams was played out amid crumbling castles, rocky promontories, moon-lit lakes and ghost-ridden abbeys, exulting in humankind's tenuous grasp on reality, either mental or physical. In this curious literary movement we can detect the ancestry of the ghost story (Sir Walter Scott, whose romantic historical adventures were suffused with the mood of the Gothic, was one of the first great writers of the ghost story), the horror novel (in a direct line through the great American exponent of gloomy terror, Edgar Allan Poe), and science fiction.

Frankenstein or The Modern Prometheus (1818) by Mary Wollstonecraft Shelley clearly has elements of the Gothic novel. Its origins lie in a competition to write a ghost story (a competition which also saw the creation of Dr John Polidori's *The Vampyre* (1819)). Its settings are precisely those wild places where nature is at its most raw, the Alps, the Arctic wastes, which are so beloved of the romantic imagination. The creature is a thing meant to instil in us both pity and terror, emotions the Romantics played on freely to express the

9

inexpressible. The creature is indeed manufactured out of corpses, an apt symbol of the transience of life. Above all, when Victor Frankenstein reports he "collected the instruments of life around me, that I might infuse a spark of being into the lifeless thing that lay at my feet", a spark translated in the films as a lightning bolt, it encapsulates everything the Gothics felt about power, transcendence and the mutability of human life.

It is the ways in which *Frankenstein* differs from the typical Gothic novel, however, that make it interesting. This is not a novel that progresses through dark shadows and hints of the supernatural but through cold logic and scientific experiment. Victor Frankenstein is a student who learns to reject the old beliefs in favour of modern empiricism. The practical experiments of her age were clearly in Mary Shelley's mind when she wrote the novel; she would have been aware of Ben Franklin's experiments with lightning, the theories of Erasmus Darwin, the galvanism that had made a dead frog jerk with apparent life. The notion that lightning might bring life would fit comfortably within the scientific thinking of her age. The creature might be a nameless terror, a golem arisen from the darkest parts of the Gothic imagination, but the nature of his birth is rational, reasonable, scientific.

To claim on the strength of this, as Brian Aldiss does, that *Frankenstein* is the first science fiction novel is perhaps to overstate the case. It lies somewhere on that line of progress which links early tales of the fantastic with modern tales of science fiction; but on that line *Frankenstein* is as far removed from the science fiction of, say, Jeff Noon as it is from the fantasy of Thomas Malory. Nevertheless, *Frankenstein* does mark a turning point within the history of science fiction, a moment of change as vital and as far reaching in its effects as the career of H.G. Wells a hundred years later or John W. Campbell's editorship of *Astounding* another half-century on.

Mary Shelley was twenty when *Frankenstein* was first published, and she earned her living by writing throughout the rest of her life. Much of what she wrote bore the effects of the Gothic, and one later novel, *The Last Man* (1826), which tells of humankind wiped out by plague at the end of the twenty-first century, is clearly science fictional amid the Gothic gloom. Yet it was with *Frankenstein* that she made her greatest impact, mostly through the stage adaptations which started to appear within a few years of the novel being published, and it was with *Frankenstein* that the history of science fiction in the nineteenth century properly begins.

In truth, though, it was some time before much came of this start.

The Victorian age was a time of expansion and boundless optimism. The maps of the day coloured Britain's Empire and possessions in red, and the most important corners of the world all had their areas of red. Technological wonders were being introduced in abundance; the Great Exhibition at the Crystal Palace was a glittering display of the future here today. True, some inventions such as Charles Babbage's difference engine didn't seem to lead anywhere, and some theories, notably Charles Darwin's theory of the origin of species, did upset the safe, conventional view of the world but in general men, and Englishmen in particular, were confident masters of all they beheld.

Yet none of this translated into the literature. For most of the nineteenth century little of any lasting worth that might be termed science fiction was published. Fantasy fared better: in *Idylls of the King* by Alfred, Lord Tennyson the Gothic fascination with all things medieval found its finest literary expression. King Arthur was again placed at the heart of British fantasy, and the fascination was translated wholesale into the Pre-Raphaelite movement as images from Tennyson's poetry were transformed into paintings by Burne-Jones and Dyce and photographs by Julia Margaret Cameron. Arthur's cultural position was confirmed by William Morris, who not only published an exquisite edition of *Le Morte d'Arthur* at his

A Short History of British Fantasy and Science Fiction

Kelmscott Press, but also wrote a series of fantasies, notably *The Wood Beyond the World* (1894) and *The Well at the World's End* (1896), which merged the Victorian love of the medieval with Morris's own idealistic socialism. Morris's work, notably in its influence upon another medieval scholar, J.R.R. Tolkien, can be seen to be paving the way for modern heroic fantasy, but fantasy was also set off in a different direction by the publication of two books by an Oxford mathematician. *Alice's Adventures in Wonderland* (1865) and *Through the Looking Glass and What Alice Found There* (1871) by Lewis Carroll (Charles Lutwidge Dodgson) were enchanting dreamscapes full of characters (the White Rabbit, the Queen of Hearts, the Mad Hatter, Tweedledum and Tweedledee) who have been staples of children's literature ever since. They were also witty conflations of logical paradoxes and puzzles, much as notions of time running backwards and telepathy were entertainingly explored in his *Sylvie and Bruno* (1867) and its sequel, *Sylvie and Bruno Concluded* (1893). These books had the suitably paradoxical result that fantasy since then has been seen both as literature for children and as literature that can be intellectually challenging. The Victorian age also saw an interest in fairy stories, inspired probably by the work of writers and collectors such as Hans Christian Andersen, the Brothers Grimm and, later, Andrew Lang, but finding very different expression in the works of George MacDonald, particularly *Phantastes* (1858) and *Lilith* (1895), and Oscar Wilde, *The Happy Prince and Other Tales* (1888). Yet another major contribution to British fantasy came late in the century when an Irish journalist picked up on an idea already used by Polidori. *Dracula* (1897), by Bram Stoker, conjured illogical monsters from the darkest corners of the mind, then played to Victorian sensibilities by suggesting the equation of horror with sexuality. It was an immortal creation (none of Stoker's other potboilers ever came close in execution or effect) and the vampire continues to be one of the dominant figures of twentieth century horror, mostly, as with *Frankenstein* before it, as a result of cinematic appearances.

These were exciting times for English literature, and many of the greatest writers of the day were happy to venture into the fantastic. Jane Austen wrote a satire of all things Gothic in *Northanger Abbey* (1818). Charles Dickens didn't just create a new career for himself on the public reading circuit with his immensely popular *A Christmas Carol* (1843) but also wrote one of the most chilling and most widely anthologised of all ghost stories in "The Signalman" (1866), while other writers such as Elizabeth Gaskell, J.S. LeFanu, Wilkie Collins and Amelia B. Edwards were helping to give the English ghost story the shape it would eventually achieve around the end of the century. Even Thomas Hardy's novels of rural life were full of the awareness of new sciences like geology and palaeontology. Yet science fiction itself languished, except for one or two curious exceptions. One of these, *Strange Case of Dr Jekyll and Mr Hyde* (1886) by Robert Louis Stevenson, took the *Frankenstein* theme and located the monster within ourselves, a notion that would find many imitators over the years to come; though, like Mary Shelley's original, this was a work of science fiction that would find itself transformed into horror as soon as it made the transition to the silver screen. The other notable exception was *Flatland: A Romance of Many Dimensions* (1884) by Edwin A. Abbott, which, like Lewis Carroll's work before it, used fantasy to express an academic, mathematical notion.

Only in the last quarter of the century did two linked themes emerge to give a fresh impetus to futuristic fiction. Both were perhaps symptomatic of the end of an era, expressing the first tentative doubts about Britain's continuing pre-eminence on the world stage. The first theme, looking across the Channel at Bismarck's efforts to unite Germany, particularly in the wake of the unexpectedly quick defeat of France in the Franco-Prussian War of 1870-71, found nervous expression in stories of invasion. *The Invasion of England: A Possible Tale of*

Future Times (1870) by Alfred Bate Richards, *The Battle of Dorking* (1871) by George T. Chesney, *For England's Sake* (1889) by Robert Cromie, *The Great War of 189–: A Forecast* (1893) by Philip H. Colomb, *The Great War in England in 1897* (1894) by William Le Queux: all these and more were intended primarily as spirited appeals to British patriotism, stirring demands to face the foreign menace. They never looked far into the future, and indeed these warning shots generated the first great spy novel of the twentieth century, *The Riddle of the Sands* (1903) by Erskine Childers.

The second theme, providing a parallel to these stories filled with the spectre of modern weapons of mass destruction, was the re-emergence of utopianism. These visions of an ideal way to live now had two new weapons in their armoury: Darwin's notion of the survival of the fittest and Marx's notion of historical, social progress, both now filtering, in one form or another, into popular consciousness. On the same day that Blackwoods Magazine published *The Battle of Dorking*, Edward Bulwer-Lytton's *The Coming Race* (1871) appeared. With the proposition that a superior underground race would supplant our own, Lytton was serving notice that the new utopias might be as uncomfortable as the invasion stories (and in the name of that race, "Vril-ya", and in their life force "vril", he was bequeathing to the world a word that would later re-appear in the popular British beef extract, "Bovril"). Other utopias quickly followed. Some, such as Samuel Butler's *Erewhon* (1872), re-established the use of utopias in satire; others, such as W.H. Hudson's *A Crystal Age* (1887) or Richard Jefferies' *After London* (1885) which presaged S. Fowler Wright and later Richard Cowper in turning England into an archipelago, advocated a return to a pastoral world; while still others, notably William Morris's *News from Nowhere* (1890), simply celebrated the anticipated success of a socialist ideal.

These themes came together in the work of perhaps the single most important writer in the history of science fiction. H.G. Wells was born in 1866 to the sort of lower middle class family he would later write about in works like *Kipps* (1905) and *The History of Mr Polly* (1910). Economic necessity forced him to become apprenticed to a draper, but he went on to win a scholarship to the Normal School of Science (later Imperial College) where he studied under T.H. Huxley, one of the leading Darwinists of his day, who clearly inspired Wells in many of the ideas he would espouse throughout his life. He began to dabble first with scientific journalism, then with short stories, then in 1895 published the first of a string of scientific romances which would change the nature of the genre.

The Time Machine (1895) presented, at best, a very ambiguous utopia, with the gentle Eloi and bestial Morlocks owing much to the notions of coming races presented by other Darwinian writers, such as Bulwer-Lytton. But in the scene at the end of time, when the traveller watches a strange tentacled creature (perhaps not unlike Wells' later Martians) on a desolate beach, Wells took the Darwinian notion of evolution farther than any writer had hitherto dared to the entropic ending of life. And in the invention of the time machine itself he not only created one of the most fruitful strands in the future history of science fiction, he also drew a line once and for all under those utopian futures reached by something more akin to dreaming than by rational means. Wells, a socialist who loved society, a Fabian who relished the wealth his fame brought him, returned time and again to creating utopias throughout his career, but they were always ambivalent. In *The Sleeper Wakes* (1898, revised 1910) a man from 1897 awakes from a cataleptic fit in 2100 to find what appears to be a paradise, though he soon finds himself playing a messianic role. The better society in *In the Days of the Comet* (1906) needs the cataclysmic effect of a comet's tail to overcome the human obstacles to change. Utopias featured also in *A Modern Utopia* (1905) and *Men Like Gods* (1923), but Wells had quickly come to recognise that his ideals could only be achieved by overturning everything that stood in its way and creating a World State. He saw this eventuality as inevitable, and in his last and largest exercise in utopian thinking, *The Shape of Things to Come* (1933), he took as his starting point the First World War and traced the birth of a benign world state through the traumas of war and destruction.

The other theme which runs through much of Wells' work is concerned with invasion and war, and finds its first and finest expression in *The War of the Worlds* (1898). Again he took a common subject for the science fiction of the day, the paranoia about invasion, and gave it a truly novel twist with the security of the Home Counties menaced not by Germans but by the cold intelligence of an alien race. Other races had appeared in fiction before, but these were the first true alien invaders in literature, and again Wells had set a precedent which science fiction has followed ever since. In one of the most famous endings in the genre, it is earthly bacteria rather than human firepower which defeat the invaders; the Martian superiority in weapons remains until the end. This fascination with the destructive potential of advanced weaponry crops up frequently in Wells' work, most notably in "The Land Ironclads" (1903) which introduced the idea of the tank a decade before they were actually created for use in the First World War, *The War in the Air* (1908) which envisioned the military power of aircraft less than five years after the Wright Brothers first flew, and *The World Set Free* (1914) which predicted atomic war thirty years before the Manhattan Project.

Wells was one of the most influential writers ever to work in science fiction. His impact on the genre was immeasureable, for he either established or developed most of the themes that have formed the bulk of science fiction ever since. As well as time travel and alien invasion he presented us with notions of flight to other worlds in *The First Men in the Moon* (1901), invisibility in *The Invisible Man* (1897), and the genetic engineering of beasts into men in *The Island of Dr Moreau* (1896). Although much of his most inventive work appeared in these early novels, he continued to write science fiction throughout his career alongside his social novels, popular histories, experiments in autobiography and more. Despite the fact that the dividing lines between high and low culture were being set in concrete by critics such as Leavis during Wells' lifetime, it seems to have had little or no effect on either the popular or critical reception for his work. At one point in 1902 his friend Henry James, doyen of high culture, even suggested collaboration on a novel about Mars: Wells sensibly turned down the idea. Along with a wealth of new ideas, Wells bequeathed a vigorous demotic language to science fiction which would have been ill-suited to the self-conscious prose of James.

Chapter Two

Glimpsing the Future

IN 1886, CHARLES Howard Hinton published a collection of articles and stories called *Scientific Romances*. The term "science fiction" had already been used (in *A Little Earnest Book upon a Great Old Subject* (1851) by William Wilson, referring to Richard Henry Horne's *The Poor Artist* (1849)), but it was scientific romance which became accepted as the name for the nascent genre. Brian Stableford has characterised scientific romance as "a story which is built around something glimpsed through a window of possibility from which scientific discovery has drawn back the curtain." But the key element of the term is "romance". These were stories written in the romantic tradition, their main impulse being to generate broad emotions of awe and terror, and it was a much broader genre than its depiction as an early form of science fiction might suggest. True, the heart of the genre and one of the significant elements in its popular success, was the work of H.G. Wells, but scientific romance was catholic enough to embrace the adventure stories of H. Rider Haggard (notably *King Solomon's Mines* (1886) and *She* (1887)), the voices prophesying war whose finest expression was probably *When William Came* (1913) by H.H. Munro ("Saki"), and William Hope Hodgson's *The House on the Borderland* (1908) which introduced a cosmic perspective to supernatural horror (and which would influence H.P. Lovecraft) and *The Night Land* (1912) which fused the supernatural and the scientific in a bleak vision of the future.

Few of the writers of scientific romance could match Wells' scientific training. The genre seemed mostly to attract free thinkers who saw in it a chance to express their political or religious views. Darwinism, in a variety of interpretations, had become the intellectual cornerstone of the age. Whether execrated by those who propounded a religious viewpoint or expounded by those who saw themselves as modern or scientific, it underpinned much of the moral and political debate during the latter years of Queen Victoria's reign. Evolution became a handy notion that was taken up with enthusiasm (if not always with much rigour or comprehension) by early writers of scientific romance such as George Griffiths, William Le Queux and M.P. Shiel. Shiel in particular played with notions of Social Darwinism when he jumped on the future war bandwagon with such xenophobic tales as *The Yellow Danger* (1898), *The Yellow Wave* (1905) and *The Yellow Peril* (originally published as *The Dragon*, 1913). This, it should be remembered, was the time when Japan was shocking the Great

Powers of the day with the speed of its emergence onto the world stage, culminating in its defeat of Russia in the war of 1904, which went directly against all contemporary notions of military might and white superiority. Of course, the racism in Shiel's books was no more than was common in the works of many more respectable writers of the time, and he did delight in shocking his audience, but even Shiel's defender, Brian Stableford, has to admit to "a certain amount of anti-Semitic comment" in one of his best works, *The Lord of the Sea* (1901), though the novel also has religious overtones (the emergence of a new (Jewish!) Messiah) which are echoed in his most successful book, *The Purple Cloud* (1901). This tells the story of a new Adam and Eve and their struggle to survive and reconcile themselves with events after a poisonous purple gas has wiped out the rest of humankind.

The emergence of scientific romance during the 1890s was part of a much wider flourishing of popular fiction. To an extent this was due to educational reforms in the 1870s which had increased literacy in Britain, but more important was probably the decline of the triple-decker novel. For most of the century there had been an artificial distinction between the serious novel, generally published in three volumes, and popular "penny dreadfuls", but cheaper production methods finally ousted the triple-decker and made more books more widely available. At the same time a new generation of magazines, such as *Pearson's* and *The Strand*, started to appear, hungry for cheap fiction to fill their pages. Writers found they could now make a living turning out quick stories on demand, and since ever more lurid tales were demanded by editors to increase sales, it is easy to see why scientific romance in particular soon became associated with poorly written hack work. (It was against this background that academic critics like F.R. Leavis, trying to identify the best in literature, found it easy to dismiss genre fiction in general as among the worst.)

But such distinctions were still to come. As this upswelling of popular culture occurred there were virtually no distinctions between genres, and authors, whether their appeal was high, middle or low brow, were happy to move from one form to another. Arthur Conan Doyle's first success, for instance, was with historical adventures such as *The White Company* (1891) and *The Exploits of Brigadier Gerard* (1896). He went on to achieve overwhelming popularity with his stories of Sherlock Holmes, probably the most widely-known character in the history of English literature. He had flirted with scientific romance as early as *The Doings of Raffles Haw* (1891), and returned to the genre with the Professor Challenger stories, starting with *The Lost World* (1912). This first Challenger story, which tells of prehistoric creatures discovered on an isolated South American plateau, was something of a *jeu d'esprit*. Later stories, such as *The Poison Belt* (1913) in which the Earth passes through a belt of "luminiferous ether" thought to be poisonous (an echo of Shiel's purple cloud), "When the World Screamed" (1929) in which a drill pierces the Earth's crust and wounds the Gaia-like living creature our planet is, and the non-Challenger novel *The Maracot Deep* (1927) which concerns the occult effects of the discovery of relics from Atlantis, all clearly had a more serious intent.

Doyle was in many ways the archetypal professional writer of his day, ready to turn his hand to any type of story, but he wasn't the only one doing this. Other writers with less lasting appeal were similarly protean. William Le Queux, who built his career almost exclusively on stories about the German threat (to the extent that he even claimed to have been a spy himself) also published lost race fantasies such as *Zoraida* (1896) and tales of the occult such as *Stolen Souls* (1895), while George Griffith wrote historical novels such as *The Rose of Judah* (1898) as well as his scientific romances such as *The Angel of the Revolution* (1893).

At the opposite end of the literary spectrum writers recognised as among the finest of their generation would essay the occasional fantastic tale, often as an ironic commentary upon the work of H.G. Wells, as happened with G.K. Chesterton's *The Napoleon of Notting Hill* (1904) and E.M. Forster's "The Machine Stops" (1909). An even more impressive example of this is found in the work of Rudyard Kipling, whose stories and poems were the stirring voice of late Victorian consciousness. Many of his most successful stories crossed whatever genre boundaries there were, with fairy story and fantasy entering into the magical or allegorical worlds of *Puck of Pook's Hill* (1906), *Rewards and Fairies* (1910), *The Jungle Book* (1894) and *The Just So Stories* (1902), while he made a triumphant contribution to the history of scientific romance with *With the Night Mail* (1909), one of the finest stories in the genre. This subtle examination of the effects of air travel on the world uses postmodern techniques *avant la lettre* in the way newspaper advertisements are used to carry the main world-building weight of the story. These were not surreptitious entries into the genre but part of an ongoing tradition of what we might call "mainstream" writers making use of the opportunities of genre material, often for satiric purposes. Writers like Aldous Huxley, J.B. Priestley and George Orwell would follow over the next few years, while Henry James, perhaps the most influential man of letters of his generation, had already led the way with his ghost story *The Turn of the Screw* (1898).

This story, which tells of a governess confronting the pernicious influence of two ghosts upon her charges (or of the psychosis of either the governess or the children, depending on interpretation) is one of the most subtle ghost stories ever written. The critic Tzvetan Todorov, in his groundbreaking study of fantastic literature, defined the fantastic as literature which required the reader to hesitate between a natural and supernatural explanation of the events described. "The fantastic occupies the duration of this uncertainty" but as soon as we opt for one explanation or another the story becomes a representative of neighbouring genres, either the uncanny or the marvellous. Todorov seemed to identify only one story which shows that "hesitation" which he considers the mark of the true fantasy: *The Turn of the Screw*. The plot of *The Turn of the Screw* was suggested to James by his friend E.W. Benson, Archbishop of Canterbury, and two of the Archbishop's sons also play a significant part in this history. R.H. Benson, a Roman Catholic monk, wrote *Lord of the World* (1907), one of the finest of the scientific romances which featured the Day of Judgement as the end point of human progress. His brother E.F. Benson, later famous for his social comedies about Miss Mapp and Lucia, and the person who took over Henry James's Lamb House in Rye, was one of the writers responsible for the great days of the traditional English ghost story. Along with Barry Pain (a humorous writer who also ventured into scientific romance as with *An Exchange of Souls* (1911)), Jerome K. Jerome (whose greatest fame came with comedies such as *Three Men in a Boat* (1889)), E. Nesbit (best remembered now for her delicate and wonderful children's fantasies such as *Five Children and It* (1902) and especially M.R. James (Provost of Eton and author of scholarly studies), E.F. Benson helped to create the English ghost story as it is remembered today. The greatest of these was, of course, M.R. James, whose collections, *Ghost Stories of an Antiquary* (1904) and *More Ghost Stories of an Antiquary* (1911), established the idea that ghost stories involved academics caught up in experiences beyond their understanding in remote landscapes or ruinous old houses as fraught with atmosphere and meaning as anything conjured up by the Gothics. Stories such as "The Mezzotint" (1904) in which the purchaser of a picture watches helplessly as a strange figure moves across the landscape and into the house that is the subject of the picture only to leave later with the sense of some terrible but unidentifiable menace; or "Oh Whistle and I'll Come to Thee, My Lad" (1904) in which something unidentifiable pursues the hapless narrator across a deserted beach, then rises up as a figure of crumpled bedclothes, are as haunting, tenebrous and darkly romantic as any in the English language.

Having achieved its apotheosis in the works of Henry James, M.R. James and E.F. Benson, the English ghost story has tended to languish throughout the rest of the century. Occasional writers, notably Ramsey Campbell, have demonstrated that there is life in the tradition yet, but anthologists from Cynthia Asquith to Peter Haining, Hugh Lamb, Michael Cox, Richard Dalby and Rosemary Pardoe, have tended to be retrospective. The efforts, in particular, of Cox, Dalby and Pardoe has seen a revival of interest in the English ghost story during the 1980s and '90s, but this has not so far translated into a significant flowering of new writing other than in the small presses.

In the days of its greatest triumph, however, the traditional ghost story was already transmuting into something closer to what we might term, in more modern parlance, dark fantasy or even horror. There are suggestions of this change in the work, for instance, of May Sinclair (*Uncanny Stories* (1923)) and Walter de la Mare, now better known as a poet but also the author of weird short stories such as "Seaton's Aunt" (1923) with its suggestion of malignant vampirism. There was a strong occult influence in the works of Algernon Blackwood also, especially in stories such as *The Centaur* (1911) and the adventures of his psychic detective, John Silence, though Blackwood's interests ranged widely from reincarnation (*The Bright Messenger* (1921)) to the theory of serial universes proposed by J.W. Dunne ("The Willows" (1907)). The most interesting and in some respects the most modern of these fantasists, however, was Arthur Machen. In *The Great God Pan* (1894), for instance, the story starts with a young woman who glimpses Pan while undergoing brain surgery, then dies. Years later a young girl in rural Wales is the focus for terrifying events, and later still a society beauty drives her husband and other men around her to horrifying deaths, all the events linking back to that deathbed meeting with Pan. During the First World War Machen wrote two of his most famous stories: as in much of his work, "The Great Return" (1915) is a variation on the Grail story, while "The Bowmen" (1914) tells how English archers from Agincourt appeared to help the English Expeditionary Force in the early days of the war. This story (collected in *The Bowmen and Other Legends of the War*, 1915) almost instantly gave rise to the legend of the Angels of Mons which is still sometimes quoted as a genuine visionary experience.

The First World War, of course, changed everything. H.H. Munro and William Hope Hodgson both died during the war. Arthur Conan Doyle lost a son, became a devout follower of spiritualism (a belief all too evident in the Professor Challenger story *The Land of Mist* (1926)) and fell volubly for the deception of the Cottingley Fairies. Even H.G. Wells turned briefly to religion. Society also was different. Women who had gone to the factories and farms to help out during the war were not going to quietly resume their old social role, especially not in a land depleted of men. Under the superficial gaiety of the 1920s was a despair and an unrest that came out sporadically, for instance in the General Strike of 1926, then more devastatingly during the Depression of the 1930s, punctuated by the famous Hunger Marches. The leading writers of the day, for instance Virginia Woolf in *Mrs Dalloway* (1925), used new modernist techniques such as stream of consciousness to explore shattered personalities and a shattered social world. Even the popular writers had to change, and not just because the reliable pre-war market for short stories was drying up.

The old beliefs that fiction could hold a simple mirror to the world, that truth was easily encompassed and that the stiff-upper-lip of English imperialism was enough to see any hero through any situation, were no longer sufficient. Mainstream fiction took on a grim aspect, experimenting with new styles and devices to represent a new uncertainty. Along with this

17

there was a demand for escapism which led to the resurgence of fantasy in the years immediately after the war. The years before the war had seen early stories by Lord Dunsany and, perhaps more significantly, Kenneth Grahame's The Wind in the Willows (1908). This was not the first animal fantasy, but it was the most enduring and, in chapters such as "The Piper at the Gates of Dawn" which merged the fantasy with an animistic theism, and which has lent its title to many other works since (most notably the story by Richard Cowper), it was also the most influential. After the war, however, such a merging of imagination and belief acquired a new impetus. Dunsany, after spurning fantasy during the war, returned to the genre with some of his strongest works, notably The King of Elfland's Daughter (1924) whose vividly described imaginary landscape was influential on the heroic fantasy that followed. E.R. Eddison successfully used mythologies other than the usual Arthurian matter in novels such as The Worm Ouroboros (1922). In many ways the most unusual of the post-war fantasists was David Lindsay, whose first and most successful novel, A Voyage to Arcturus (1920), effectively combined fantasy and scientific romance in a story of an alien world which externalised the metaphysical adventures of the protagonist.

If the 1920s saw fantasy flourishing, scientific romance languished. The mood of the country and economic circumstances were both against the new genre. Whereas in America the flourishing pulp magazines proved a perfect breeding ground for scientifiction, or science fiction as it soon became known; in Britain the magazines were in decline. In America, little touched by the war, the post-war years saw the country combining a new economic dominance with political isolation, which made it ready for an outward-looking optimistic genre which lauded the perceived American virtues. In Britain the post-war economy was in ruins, trading partners, allies and former enemies in Europe were in even worse state. The few works of scientific romance that appeared during the decade, The People of the Ruins (1920) by Edward Shanks, The Clockwork Man (1923) by E.V. Odle, Lest Ye Die (1928, a revised version of Theodore Savage, 1922) by Cicely Hamilton, give sufficient clues in their title to how they matched the mood of the country.

Of these post-war scientific romancers, the most successful was S. Fowler Wright, whose writing was probably responsible for the common American view of British science fiction as down beat and depressing. Fowler Wright saw few redeeming features in humankind, and held out little hope for their future. In what was probably his most famous novel, The World Below (1929) (which actually consisted of his first scientific romance, The Amphibians (1925), along with its sequel) he echoes Wells' first novel by sending a time traveller far beyond man's disappearance from Earth, only to reveal the bestiality of humankind in comparison to the gentle Amphibians, while in Deluge (1927) and its sequel Dawn (1931) he used what was shortly to become the most characteristic form of British science fiction, the catastrophe story, to give full dramatic rein to his pessimism. Universal flooding causes the Cotswolds to become a tiny chain of islands (a scenario that would be echoed in Christopher Priest's A Dream of Wessex (1977) and Richard Cowper's The Road to Corlay (1978)) and here the few survivors try to make a home in a hostile landscape for which civilisation, which Fowler Wright identifies with all that is evil in mankind, has ill prepared them.

Fowler Wright's popularity started to decline just as scientific romance began a resurgence during the 1930s. The reasons for this are complex. The worldwide depression that followed the Wall Street Crash of 1929 created a need for escapist literature and much of the fantastic writing of this time was little more than colourful adventure. But the economic conditions also stirred the predominantly socialist inclinations of writers of scientific romance (Wells, for instance, returned to the genre at this time). This was amplified by the rise of fascism in Italy, Germany and later Spain which set writers either looking ahead to a better future for mankind, or despairing of human nature. At the same time the 1920s had seen a plethora of popular essays by scientists, philosophers, historians and other intellectuals, many of which had contained a serious contemplation of the future, or of the possibilities that science opened up for us. Notable among these were *Essays of a Biologist* (1923) by Julian Huxley, *Daedalus: or, Science and the Future* (1924) by J.B.S. Haldane which was answered by Bertrand Russell in his more cynical *Icarus: or, the Future of Science* (1925), and *The World, the Flesh and the Devil* (1929) by J.D. Bernal, while other, more ambitious, books such as *Decline of the West* (1918-22) by Oswald Spengler and *An Experiment with Time* (1927) by J.W. Dunne also contributed to the intellectual framework and stimulus for scientific romances and fantastic literature both within and outwith the genre.

J.B. Priestley, for instance, was influenced by Dunne's ideas in his use of time and alternative realities in plays such as *Dangerous Corner* (1932), *Time and the Conways* (1937), *I Have Been Here Before* (1937) and *An Inspector Calls* (1945). Such notions about time also came out in a curious and inventive collection of essays by historians and writers such as G.K. Chesterton, Hilaire Belloc, Harold Nicolson and Andre Maurois, *If It Had Happened Otherwise* (1932) edited by J.C. Squire. Although inspired by a 1907 essay by the highly respected historian G.M. Trevelyan, "If Napoleon had Won the Battle of Waterloo", this collection was really the first popular appearance of alternate histories, and the star of the show was undoubtedly Winston Churchill who gave an extra twist to the notion with his essay "If Lee had Not Won the Battle of Gettysburg". Nevertheless, despite the efforts of Priestley and Squire, it would be many years yet before alternate histories really became an established part of British science fiction.

Another mainstream writer inspired by the essays of the 1920s and the politics of the 1930s to venture into scientific romance was Aldous Huxley. Then best known for mainstream novels such as *Crome Yellow* (1921) and *Antic Hay* (1923) which captured the Jazz Age in Britain as his contemporary, F. Scott Fitzgerald, was doing in America, he wrote *Brave New World* (1932) in part as a response to the essays by his brother Julian and his friend Haldane, and in part as a satire on the scientific world state. Like Wells' before him, Huxley's utopia is equivocal, wary of scientific progress as a threat to individuality and freedom but not actually condemning it outright. This ambiguous utopia is now seen as one of the seminal works of British science fiction, one of the handful of books that has progressed so far into the popular imagination that it is recognised even by those who would not otherwise read science fiction. And having once discovered the genre, Huxley would return to it again and again throughout his career, mostly with utopian works such as *Ape and Essence* (1948) and *Island* (1962), though never again with the same power or success.

John Cowper Powys' huge rambling novels provide a counterpoint to the works of Olaf Stapledon, putting a complex structure at the service of a distinctive *weltanschauung*. But where Stapledon tended towards impersonality, Powys, in novels such as *A Glastonbury Romance* (1932), *Morwyn* (1937) and *The Brazen Head* (1956), sought to be ever more personal as his large casts of characters represented the diversity of his pluralistic world view.

The fantastic, in fact, was so accepted a part of the popular imagination that works from other genres regularly used themes or devices borrowed from fantasy or scientific romance. The crime novelist Margery Allingham, for instance, used supernatural elements in *Look to the Lady* (1931) (and a science-fictional mind reading device in *The Mind Readers* (1965)) while Dorothy L. Sayers edited *Great Short Stories of Detection, Mystery and Horror* (1928, 1931, 1934) as if the genres were interchangeable. The humorous writer P.G. Wodehouse stole the notion of swapped personalities from F. Anstey (*Vice Versa* (1882)) for his novel *Laughing Gas* (1936).

The 1930s saw war in the Far East and in Spain, and war clouds gathering over Nazi Germany. The ruins of the First World War were still fresh in people's minds, and the Depression and the Jarrow March can have done little to suggest that a better life was, or could be, on the horizon. So it is small wonder that the scientific romances of the time tended to share Fowler Wright's pessimism. Neil Bell's *The Seventh Bowl* (1930, as by "Miles") predicts the Gas War of 1940, *Three Go Back* (1932) and *Gay Hunter* (1934) by J. Leslie Mitchell (now better known for his mainstream novels of Scottish life written under the pseudonym Lewis Grassic Gibbon) both find civilisation corrupting, John Gloag's *Tomorrow's Yesterday* (1932) compares the destructiveness of human civilisation unfavourably to a new race evolved from cats, Katharine Burdekin in *Swastika Night* (1937) looks forward to a Nazi dominated future in which women are breeding animals.

However the one writer who, above all others, set humanity as no more than a small speck within the vastness of space and time, was Olaf Stapledon. After Wells he is probably the most influential figure in the history of British science fiction, though his work, often devoid of any real character or plot, stands outside not only the main stream of British science fiction but of British literature in general.

In his first novel, *Last and First Men* (1930), Stapledon catalogues not just the fall of our own civilisation (unleashed by the nuclear destruction of Lundy Island), but the races of men who come after, including those who terraform planets and those who transform themselves to live on Neptune. Remorselessly, civilisations rise and fall, some superior to ourselves, others inferior, leading across two billion years to the wisdom of the Eighteenth Men, yet always the spiritual quest, the great theme that runs through all of Stapledon's work, remains unfulfilled. A similar time scale and a similar witnessing of processes that are indifferent to our humanity is provided by perhaps his finest novel, *Star Maker* (1937). In this work a human observer is swept up into the heavens to witness cosmic forces and alien races, each in some way reflecting aspects of Stapledon's own ethical and spiritual musings, until at the climax he faces the pitiless Star Maker.

Stapledon's other works do not have this impersonal grandeur and, perhaps because of that, seem like lesser works. Even at their best, for instance his story of a superman, *Odd John* (1935), his attempts at characterisation reveal the shortcomings in his writing. His work was clearly at its best when it was little more than lightly fictionalised philosophical speculation about matters beyond the normal human ken or scale. Though in *Sirius* (1944), in which the narrator and central character is a dog with enhanced intelligence, the non-human perspective allows him to make his point about human violence and limitations with something of the old intellectual freedom.

Although Stapledon continued writing until his death in 1950, these four books, along with *Last Men in London* (1932), constitute his most significant works. After the Second World War his work would be largely forgotten until the 1960s, though it would have a major impact upon the genre, not least through its influence on Arthur C. Clarke.

Chapter Three

The Other Side of the Dream

IN THE DECADE and a half following the Second World War four writers, two in fantasy and two in science fiction, would represent the parting of the ways that both these genres now faced. There were other writers, of course, many of them, for the 1950s saw one of the periodic booms in British fantastic literature, and some would achieve greater prominence, but somehow Mervyn Peake and J.R.R. Tolkien, John Wyndham and Arthur C. Clarke are emblematic of the choices that faced fantasy and science fiction respectively in the years after 1945.

Wyndham and Clarke both sprang from the same tradition. In the mid-1930s American pulp science fiction magazines became more easily available in this country (it was said they were shipped over as ballast in merchant ships). As a result, people started to develop a taste for American science fiction as opposed to British scientific romance. Fan groups were founded (the first science fiction convention was held in Leeds in 1937) and writers such as John Russell Fearn, Eric Frank Russell and William F. Temple sold stories to American magazines which copied American science fiction stories very closely in tone and manner. Some British writers would continue to write principally for American magazines throughout their careers, notably Russell who could be regarded as a de facto American author – he was the first British writer to win a Hugo Award, for his short story "Allamagoosa" (1955). John Wyndham, writing as John Beynon Harris, part of his extraordinarily flexible name (his full name, John Wyndham Parkes Lucas Beynon Harris, provided him with a remarkable collection of pseudonyms and even once allowed him to collaborate with himself as John Wyndham and Lucas Parkes on *The Outward Urge* (1959)), was one of the most prominent members of this group. He sold his first story, "Worlds of Barter", to Hugo Gernsback's *Wonder Stories* in 1931. After the war, however, he took to using the John Wyndham form of his name and changed the style of his fiction. The typically British disaster story which had already developed from Wells' *The War of the Worlds* through to the pessimism of S. Fowler Wright and John Gloag was transmuted in Wyndham's hands into what Brian Aldiss would later christen the "cosy catastrophe".

As in the 1920s so in the 1940s, the economic effects of World War were different in America and Britain. In America, which had not been directly touched by the war, the ills of the Depression had been cured by the demands of the military, and the end of the war saw the

United States now unchallenged as the strongest military and economic power in the world. In Britain homes, industry and transport had been wrecked by systematic German bombing. Some of the temporary prefab housing, erected for those who had been bombed out of their homes, survives to this day, while rationing lasted well into the 1950s. Politically and militarily we were a client state of the USA, economically we were as dependent on Marshall Aid as any of the defeated nations; we may have won the war but we had lost all but the semblance of being a Great Power, and over the succeeding years we would lose what remained of our Empire as well. The immediate post-war election returned a Labour government which instituted a massive programme of reforms, from creating the National Health Service to nationalising the coal industry, but as the elation of victory faded there was a steady drift to the right again throughout the doggedly colourless 1950s. This was no time for optimism, and Wyndham's great post-war novels reflected this mood perfectly. They were middle-class stories of middle-class people who find their familiar world torn away from them, but after a series of tribulations some form of order is restored. If Wyndham domesticated the disaster that had been a staple of British scientific romance, he did so by turning it into a novel of character which had been absent from most of the British and also American science fiction of the immediate pre-war years. In novels such as *The Day of the Triffids* (1951) in which giant plants rampage through the English Home Counties, where most of the population have been blinded; *The Kraken Wakes* (1953) where the Earth is flooded, *The Chrysalids* (1955) with mutant children who develop telepathic powers after a nuclear war, and *The Midwich Cuckoos* (1957) in which aliens impregnate the women of an isolated English village, Wyndham triumphantly established a British idiom within science fiction by building on the themes and devices of scientific romance.

Wyndham's work inspired a revival of the catastrophe story, though the writers who followed did not make their work so reassuring. Most of the writers of cosy catastrophe, such as John Lymington with *The Night of the Big Heat* (1959) or *Froomb!* (1964), Charles Eric Maine with *The Tide Went Out* (1958) or John Blackburn with *The Scent of New-Mown Hay* (1958), had more verve but less style that Wyndham, though Wyndham's nearest rival, John Christopher, was at least his match as a writer and some of his best ecological disaster stories such as *The Death of Grass* (1956), *The World in Winter* (1962) and *A Wrinkle in the Skin* (1965) were probably better than anything Wyndham wrote. And Christopher in particular was more radical in the damage he inflicted on the landscape and his characters, and more realistic in the way he avoided easy solutions. Nevertheless, the catastrophe story had such an air of safeness about it that the writers of the New Wave in the 1960s ostentatiously turned their back on it. Even so, the catastrophe story has remained a key element in British science fiction, and variations on the theme have come from J.G. Ballard (*The Drowned World* (1962) and *The Crystal World* (1966), Brian Aldiss (*Greybeard* (1964) and *Earthworks* (1965)), Keith Roberts (*The Furies* (1966)), Christopher Priest (*Fugue for a Darkening Island* (1972)), M. John Harrison (*The Committed Men* (1971)), Richard Cowper (*The Twilight of Briareus* (1974)) and Emma Tennant (*The Time of the Crack* (1973)). Most recently Peter F. Hamilton has used a catastrophe as the background for *Mindstar Rising* (1993) and its sequels, though the catastrophe now seems to have shifted genre towards horror, as, for instance, in Ian Watson's *The Power* (1987) and Simon Clark's *Blood Crazy* (1995).

Arthur C. Clarke started as a fan of science fiction, but unlike Wyndham he remained faithful to the genre after the war. Whereas Wyndham set his stories predominantly in the here-and-now, predominantly in a recogniseable Britain where the only overtly science fictional intrusion came from the cause of the catastrophe which set his plots in motion, Clarke roamed through space and time, his stories as thoroughly science fictional in setting and furnishings as those of his American contemporaries Isaac Asimov and Robert A. Heinlein. So much so, indeed, that Clarke's work was seen as belonging in their school, and he steadily established a reputation for himself as one of the finest writers of sf in which technology is optimistically presented as a hope for humankind. Clarke has acknowledged, however, that one of the greatest influences on his work was the fiction of that archetypal yet curiously individual scientific romancer, Olaf Stapledon. It is easy to see that the scale and scope of Stapledon's work is echoed in Clarke's stories set deep in space or far in the future. But by far the more significant influence, and one that gives a distinctively British flavour to Clarke's work, is Stapledon's restless quest for religious significance. Clarke rids this of any of the pessimism associated with scientific romance and transforms it into a fascination with transcendence which forms a theme underlying all his best work. Ever since Wells' time traveller had met the Morlocks and the Eloi, writers of scientific romance had viewed the transformation of humanity as loss; for Clarke it represented gain. Technology was the key to the future, but there was mysticism also in what this key opened the way to.

Such a theme was central to the two novels of the early 1950s which are perhaps the best books he has ever written. In *The City and the Stars* (1956) the discovery of a space ship provides the spur for a new advance beyond the moribund far-future utopia of the enclosed city of Diaspar, while in *Childhood's End* (1953) technologically advanced aliens who appear as the demons of traditional Christian mythology prove in fact to be the agents of our next step up the spiritual and evolutionary ladder. There was a pellucid quality, a mystical intensity to these novels which was absent from most of his books which confined themselves to singing the praises of a technological future, but that quality was recaptured in his most famous work, which echoed the themes of these two novels (and which was itself based on a story from the same period, "The Sentinel" (1951)), *2001, A Space Odyssey* (1968). The film, which Clarke co-wrote with Stanley Kubrick, and Clarke's own novelisation of the script, tell of an enigmatic, featureless alien artefact which triggers the first evolutionary step of primordial man. The scene shifts to the end of this century: a giant monolith is discovered on the Moon which transmits a signal in the direction of Jupiter, and a space mission is sent towards Jupiter to investigate. One man alone survives this mission, only to be plunged into the transcendental "star gate" from which he emerges in an unforgettable image as a "star child".

Clarke's spiritual quest should not be confused with a religious instinct. In one of his most notable stories, "The Star" (1955), Britain's second Hugo winner, in which a Jesuit priest and astrophysicist discovers that the Star of Bethlehem destroyed an advanced civilisation, the revealed truths of technology are shown to be stronger than those of religion. Yet there is a distinct mystical quality in his work, notable in stories such as "The Nine Billion Names of God" (1953) which uses a computer to complete the list of all possible names of the Buddhist God, so ending God's purpose with Earth. The story famously ends with the stars going out, one by one.

It is noticeable that in all of Clarke's work aliens may be enigmatic, as for instance in his multiple-award-winner *Rendezvous with Rama* (1973) and its sequels, but they are never threatening. In fact, when they do appear they are agents for change, for advance, and while there may be a wistful feeling of loss for those who are the victims of change, as with the loss of the children in *Childhood's End*, Clarke never questions the fact that progress is a good thing. It is this which tends to separate him from contemporary American writers who, in other respects, shared his optimism; this mystical yearning for evolutionary change was absent from most American fiction during the inward-looking McCarthy years, when aliens were as often as not a blatant symbol for alienation or for the enemy.

23

There were other British writers in the American mode, such as Kenneth Bulmer, John T. Phillifent (who most commonly used the pseudonym John Rackham), and E.C. Tubb, though they rarely came close to Clarke's vision or skill, and they certainly never matched his mysticism. The immediate post-war years and the 1950s saw the emergence of British sf magazines such as *Authentic, Nebula, Science Fantasy* and, most notably, *New Worlds*, a revival of a pre-war amateur magazine, *Novae Terrae*, which turned into a professional publication under the editorship of John Carnell in 1946. These encouraged a new generation of British writers, but as the stories were often rejects from the American magazines quality wasn't always high. It didn't help that outfits such as Badger Books and *Vargo Statten Science Fiction Magazine* were calling for simple-minded space adventures, written in no time at all under a bewildering variety of pseudonyms by writers such as R. Lionel Fanthorpe and John Glasby. It is hardly surprising that, Clarke and Wyndham apart, British science fiction had no high reputation during these years, though the 1950s did see the appearance of the "Jeff Hawke" strip by Sydney Jordan in the *Daily Express* and Frank Hampson's "Dan Dare – Pilot of the Future" in *Eagle*, which did much to bring science fiction to popular awareness in this country and engendered a love of the genre in many children who continued their involvement with science fiction in the following decades.

As economic recovery progressed after the immediate post-war years, the 1950s were a time of material affluence and cultural gloom. In America this was reflected in the transformation of the lone hero into the loser and lost soul of such archetypal novels of the Eisenhower years as Jack Kerouac's *On the Road* (1957) and Alfred Bester's *Tiger! Tiger!* (1956). In Britain the comparable effect was the transformation of the social novel into the novel of social decay. This was already evident in the catastrophes of Wyndham and his fellows, but it was shown even more clearly in those novels of the period where science fiction and the mainstream met. Most powerful and famous of these works, one of the most widely-known science fiction novels ever written, was *Nineteen Eighty Four* (1949) by George Orwell. Orwell was known primarily as a journalist with a clear left-wing conscience but a growing sense of disillusion with the leaders of the left, particularly the Soviet communist party. This disillusion had already found expression in his sharp allegorical fantasy, *Animal Farm* (1945), but it was most bitterly and most frighteningly revealed in *Nineteen Eighty Four*. This novel tells the story of an everyman, Winston Smith, whose attempts to become an individual (a love affair, a developing personal conscience) bring him directly into conflict with his society, personified by Big Brother. Smith is crushingly defeated.

There is a similar aura of civilisation at the end of its tether in William Golding's first novel, *Lord of the Flies* (1954). Golding often flirted with the fantastic in his work; from *The Inheritors* (1955) an account of the triumph of Cro-Magnon over Neanderthal, which was written partly in reaction to H.G. Wells' "The Grisly Folk" (1921), to the apocalyptic allegory of *Darkness Visible* (1979) and his posthumously-published historical fantasy, *The Double Tongue* (1995), by way of his comic play *The Brass Butterfly* (1957), but *Lord of the Flies* remains probably his best known work. Set on the eve of an atomic holocaust, it tells of a group of schoolboy evacuees who are shipwrecked on a desert island and whose veneer of civilisation rapidly crumbles.

These are specifically British responses to the fears and failures of their age, but it is noticeable that when another British mainstream writer produced the first book-length critical study of science fiction at the end of the 1950s, this approach to fantastic literature was largely ignored. *New Maps of Hell* (1960) by Kingsley Amis, which consisted of lectures he delivered at Princeton University, is a groundbreaking study, but it resolutely sees science fiction according to the American pattern. Amis's hero is Frederik Pohl and the emphasis on American science fiction, particularly on hard sf, is evident also in the *Spectrum* anthology series he co-edited with Robert Conquest in the early 1960s. Curiously, however, when he came to write a science fiction novel himself with *The Alteration* (1976) he chose a format, alternate history, which owed a lot to that most British of writers Keith Roberts.

Amis finds room for only one passing reference to his distinguished predecessor, C.S. Lewis, who had already published critical essays such as "On Science Fiction" (1955) at a time when, if anything, science fiction was even more disreputable than when Amis wrote. Lewis, an Oxford academic and Christian apologist, is a pivotal figure in British fantastic fiction at mid-century. As well as writing seriously about a genre that was then little regarded by academics, he had written a trilogy of novels – *Out of the Silent Planet* (1938), *Perelandra* (1943) and *That Hideous Strength* (1945) – which belong on that cusp when scientific romance was evolving into science fiction, using planetary romance as a vehicle for religious allegory yet trying to put something of the rigour of science fiction into the accounts of Mars and Venus (and he continued to write science fiction stories for *The Magazine of Fantasy and Science Fiction* during the 1950s). The Christian message implicit in the trilogy can be more than a little overwhelming for modern readers, though it was more successfully integrated into his series of fantasies for children set in Narnia, beginning with *The Lion the Witch and the Wardrobe* (1950) and in his more pointedly allegorical fantasy, *The Screwtape Letters* (1942). Few writers of that age seen as belonging to the mainstream, or to the respectability of academia, have written so extensively and so consistently in a fantastic mode but in addition to his writings, Lewis's importance also lies in his membership of the Inklings, a circle of Oxford academics and writers who met consistently over many years and who clearly influenced one another's work. Another member of the group was Charles Williams, whose fantasies such as *Many Dimensions* (1931) and *All Hallows' Eve* (1945) have, like Lewis's, a distinctly religious bent but the one who has made the greatest and most lasting impression on fantastic literature was J.R.R. Tolkien.

The Lord of the Rings (1954-55) is, almost without question, the single most important work of fantasy ever written. In form it is a long but relatively straightforward quest narrative: the hobbit, Frodo, and his companions have a ring of power which must be destroyed. Their journey takes them through an episodic series of meetings and adventures, while the success or otherwise of their venture becomes the key to a much more wide-ranging battle between the forces of good and evil. The characterisation is little more than perfunctory, the various representatives of good and evil are highly coloured but little developed, and the book is replete with the typical middle-class attitudes of Britain in the 1950s. But the success of the book stems from the strength of the story, which maintains a fast pace with few longueurs across three substantial volumes, and the detail of the world creation.

As Merton Professor of English at Oxford University, Tolkien made a study of traditional epic narrative. Early in his career he had published an edition of *Sir Gawain and the Green Knight* (1925, with E.V. Gordon), and a lecture "On Fairy Tales" (first delivered in 1938 or 1939, though possibly predating this) would be expanded and reprinted several times over the years. This academic knowledge of myth and legend was translated wholesale into his fiction so that *The Lord of the Rings* has the rhythms and narrative simplicity of a classic myth. As a philologist, he also had a fascination with the structure and development of language, and through that the creation of societies. He had been working on his Middle-earth since the early 1920s, and most of this time was spent in devising his elven languages and the worlds that lay behind these languages. Much of this work was, of course, invisible in *The Lord of the Rings* and its predecessor, *The Hobbit* (1937), though it has emerged since his death in the enormous number of books edited by his son, Christopher Tolkien. Nevertheless, the detailed working-out of Middle-earth that underpinned *The Lord of the Rings* lent the book a vividness and a verisimilitude that help to make it such an absorbing and popular work.

In fact, it wasn't until the 1960s that Tolkien's work really achieved cult status, but since then it has been seen as the template against which all heroic fantasy is measured. *The Lord of the Rings* has inspired a host of copies, but these have tended to pick up on only the most superficial aspects of Tolkien's work: the length, the narrative structure, the secondary world building, the maps. Few, if any, have matched the 20 years of world-building which preceded writing, or the philological depth of the book. Also, it has been mostly transatlantic fantasists who have worked within Tolkien's mould; in Britain a more potent pattern was established by Mervyn Peake.

Like Tolkien, Peake's key work is in the form of a trilogy: *Titus Groan* (1946), *Gormenghast* (1950) and *Titus Alone* (1959). Unlike Tolkien, Peake did not structure his work along simple, mythic lines. There is no clear opposition between good and evil in the *Gormenghast* trilogy, but a confused and idiosyncratic self-contained world so fossilized in its structure that it is effectively without rules. In his own way, like Orwell and Golding, Peake was writing about social decay, the destruction of old verities; but the decay is within the gallery of Dickensian grotesques, with such richly symbolic names as Flay, Swelter, Steerpike and Sepulchrave, who people the novels as much as it is within the vast, crumbling architecture of Gormenghast castle. (Only in the final part of the trilogy does the scene shift to the world outside the castle, and the world Titus finds there is as dystopian as the huge and claustrophobic landscape of the castle.) The story told across these three books (and into an intended fourth volume, *Titus Awakes*, which was never completed) is the coming of age of Titus and the rise and fall of Steerpike. But these characters are often forgotten for long stretches of the books as Peake prefers to explore the foetid and exuberant landscape of his imagination more than the plot which provides the excuse for the books. It is this, perhaps, which explains why his books achieved a particular vogue among the writers of the New Wave.

Though there are no overt fantasy elements within the three books, the grim interior world of the novels, the dense visual language, and the complex amorality of the narrative have established a narrative tradition followed by other British fantasists such as Colin Greenland and M. John Harrison who reject the simple, sunny heroism of Tolkien and his progeny. (And the surreal panorama of Gormenghast castle seems a likely source for the even more massive architecture that is the setting for *Feersum Endjinn* (1994) by Iain M. Banks.)

The cult success of both Tolkien and Peake would only come with the 1960s. Of the fantasies that were published during the 1950s the most immediately successful was *The Once and Future King* (1958) by T.H. White, an ironic and often humorous reworking of the Arthurian cycle. This volume consists of three previously published novels, *The Sword in the Stone* (1938), *The Witch in the Wood* (1939, retitled "The Queen of Air and Darkness" for the omnibus edition) and *The Ill-Made Knight* (1940) plus *The Candle in the Wind* which appeared here for the first time. The originally intended ending for the sequence was rejected by White's publishers during the Second World War for its anti-war sentiments, and later appeared separately as *The Book of Merlyn* (1977). Beginning on a light note with *The Sword in the Stone*, which tells of the magical education of the young Arthur by Merlyn, the sequence becomes steadily darker in tone until by the final section, *The Candle in the Wind*, it is a haunting yet pessimistic vision of loss and decay. By incorporating deliberate anachronisms and knowing asides (Mordred's use of guns brings about the destruction of the

Round Table, Thomas Malory appears as a page boy witness to the anihilation of Arthur's dreams in the final pages of the book) and by emphasising the grimmer and more unsettling aspects of the original myth, White revived and refreshed the legend, and produced a book of genuine power and originality which stands head and shoulders above the many anodyne retellings of the Arthur story that have followed in his wake.

The Once and Future King was far from being White's only venture into the fantastic. *Mistress Masham's Repose* (1946) tells of a girl who discovers a colony of Lilliputians who have survived for two hundred years in an English country estate after being brought back by Gulliver, while *Earth Stopped* (1934) and *Gone to Ground* (1935) are linked scientific romances of survival after a catastrophe. White also wrote notable ghost stories, one of the handful of mostly mainstream writers such as Elizabeth Bowen ("The Demon Lover" (1941)), Graham Greene ("A Little Place off the Edgware Road" (1947)) and V.S. Pritchett ("A Story of Don Juan" (1952)) who contributed to a temporary revival of the genre at this time. Though the real strength of the ghost story as it drifted towards the modern horror story would be found in the work of writers such as Robert Aickman ("The Trains", 1951 and "The Stains", 1980) and L.T.C. Rolt (*Sleep No More*, 1948).

Chapter Four

After the Deluge

ON 22ND NOVEMBER 1963, the day that President John F. Kennedy was assassinated, Aldous Huxley and C.S. Lewis both died. One era had ended, a new one was about to begin.

In short order, the thirteen-year-old government of Harold Macmillan, with his complacent slogan of "You've never had it so good", and his successor, Alec Douglas-Home, was replaced by Harold Wilson's Labour government with promises of "the white heat" of technological revolution. First The Beatles then The Rolling Stones precipitated an unparalleled British dominance of popular music. The affluent society again had money to spend, and was doing so in a colourful, hip, modern world that was self-consciously distancing itself from the 1950s in the length of its hair, the shortness of its skirts, the loudness of its music. Elsewhere in the world, Gagarin and Shepard had started the conquest of space that would, in fewer years than anyone anticipated, place a man upon the Moon. The future was here, and the young were claiming it for their own with rebellion and protest and drugs and sex.

All these changes had an inevitable effect on literature. The new affluence and the younger market meant a demand for fiction that reflected or appealed to the tastes of the times, and over the course of the decade there was a growth in experimental fiction and in fiction that dealt explicitly with sex, drugs, violence and politics. No form of fiction was more radically changed by this than science fiction. The harbinger of this change was the magazine *New Worlds*.

The group of fans who, as Nova Publications, had turned *New Worlds* into a professional magazine under E.J. Carnell, was running into difficulties by 1960. Wartime import restrictions had been lifted in 1958, bringing an influx of cheap American fiction to these shores, there had also been a rise in demand for paperback books and a consequent decline in sales for old-fashioned magazines. By 1964 *New Worlds* was faltering when Carnell managed to sell the magazine, and its sister title *Science Fantasy*, to publishers Roberts and Vintner. Carnell decided to step down from the editor's chair with this change of publisher and as his successor nominated a young fan who had had a few stories published in both magazines, Michael Moorcock.

Moorcock, barely out of his teens, was enthusiastic, hyperactive, bumptious and a remarkable shrewd promoter of new ideas. From the first issue under his control, number 142,

28

May and June 1964, he proclaimed "A popular literary renaissance", a new kind of sf which would be unconventional. That was the light in which the magazine was seen almost from the start, though familiar conventional writers – E.C. Tubb, Sydney J. Bounds, Donald Malcolm – continued to appear for quite some time alongside the radical young turks Moorcock was encouraging.

The two writers who set the pace for the new *New Worlds* were both well established by this time and one, Brian Aldiss, had already won a Hugo for his *Hothouse* stories (1962). Aldiss is probably the most literarily varied and inventive writer that science fiction has produced since H.G. Wells. Even in the 1960s he was in a somewhat anomalous position vis-a-vis the genre: published by Faber and Faber, one of the most prestigious publishers of the day and not normally noted for science fiction, respectably reviewed outside the genre when science fiction was generally ignored, and moving freely in the literary establishment (it was Aldiss who engineered the famous meeting between C.S. Lewis and Kingsley Amis in 1962 and Aldiss who persuaded figures like Anthony Burgess and Marghanita Laski to support an Arts Council grant for *New Worlds* in 1967). This unusual position would sometimes put Aldiss at odds with what Moorcock was doing in *New Worlds*, and he has always had a slightly edgy relationship with science fiction as a whole. In 1987 he ringingly declared that science fiction should get back in the gutter where it belonged, at a time when his own critical reputation and his position out of that gutter were safely assured. Nevertheless his awareness of and involvement in what was happening in the literary mainstream made him an enthusiastic standard bearer for Moorcock's revolution.

More than any other science fiction writer, Aldiss has never been content to repeat himself. This has made each successive book an abrupt change of pace from what has gone before, in style and content, ambition and effect. The unifying theme, in so far as there is one, is the encouragement, as Colin Greenland puts it, "to look on our own humanity and weep". Whether his books are written in argumentative engagement with traditional sf devices – *Non-Stop* (1958) takes Robert Heinlein's generation starship of *Universe* (1941) and shows it to be a trigger for social decay rather than heroism – or with the literary experiment of his day – *Report on Probability A* (1968) imports the French *nouvelle vague* into science fiction with its obsessive gathering of data shorn of all explanation – the central image is typically of isolation rather than community. Aldiss was aware of this grim edge to his vision; in one of his finest and most lyrical stories, "The Girl and the Robot with Flowers" (1965), he has the science fiction writer gloomily disappointed with the formulaic pessimism in his work. Nevertheless, at a time when popular movements were protesting the moral and intellectual bankruptcy of politicians who had brought on the Vietnam War he could not reflect the mood of the times without concentrating on moral failure. This he did most successfully in his two novels of sexual and psychological catastrophe, *Greybeard* (1964) in which the human race has been rendered sterile by nuclear tests, and *Barefoot in the Head* (1969) in which psychotropic drugs have been used as a weapon of war disconnecting the survivors from their society.

If Aldiss's restless energy was one of the major creative inspirations for the new wave, the other came from the much less flamboyant but no less impressive source of J.G. Ballard. Like Aldiss, Ballard had already started to make a name for himself before Moorcock took over *New Worlds*, and the direction he had started on was one he would follow throughout his career. Ballard took as his theme the archetypal British device of the catastrophe story, but in the same way that Aldiss subverted traditional American sf tropes, so Ballard subverted the catastrophe. His characters embrace the breakdown of society and indeed their own mental breakdown, his novels would typically end with the protagonist setting off resolutely in the direction away from recovery, renewal and hope. Furthermore, the disaster renders the landscape surreal, from the crystalline forests of *The Crystal World* (1966) to the new river born in *The Day of Creation* (1987), and as his characters engage with this world the outer landscape comes to reflect their inner mental landscape. It is this psychological depth explored within a world running out of control that became one of the central characteristics of the British new wave, though few writers managed to achieve the subtlety that was natural in Ballard's work.

Ballard's early catastrophes presented nature gone wild, in *The Wind from Nowhere* (1962), *The Drowned World* (1962) and *The Drought* (1965), but gradually he began to incorporate popular icons into his surreal disasters. The space race, and particularly the gantries of Cape Canaveral swept by Martian sand, provided a focus for stories such as "The Cage of Sand" (1962). Rock stars and astronauts, Marilyn Monroe and J.F. Kennedy formed central images in his series of condensed novels collected as *The Atrocity Exhibition* (1970). Slowly the modern technological world took on the nature of the catastrophe, the cause of psychological and sexual disintegration. In *Crash* (1973) his protagonist embarks on an orgasmic pursuit of road crashes, in *Concrete Island* (1974) he is marooned on waste land between busy motorways and begins a battle for dominance in the curious community he finds there. Time and again in Ballard's work we see that individuals, isolated and marginalised, achieve meaning only through obsessive and often sexually motivated pursuit of the catastrophe. Later, in his superb autobiographical novel *The Empire of the Sun* (1984) and its sequel, *The Kindness of Women* (1991), he revealed how many of the familiar images in his work, empty swimming pools, crashed aircraft, have their origins in his experience as a prisoner of the Japanese while still a child.

With Aldiss pointing the way towards the style, depth and quality of the literary mainstream and Ballard providing the subject matter in the psychological exploration of what became known as "inner space", the direction followed by the writers of the British New Wave inevitably became one of literary experiment. Though much was made of William Burroughs' postmodernist cut-ups (resulting in such curiosities as "The Four-Color Problem" (1971) by Barrington Bayley and "Circularization of Condensed Conventional Straight-Line Word-Image Structures" (1969) by Michael Butterworth – not all the experiments in *New Worlds* were successful) a more potent literary inspiration came from modernist writers such as James Joyce and Virginia Woolf, especially their use of what the philosopher William James had termed the "stream of consciousness". Equally potent was the influence of Sigmund Freud, Carl Jung and R.D. Laing – this sf tended to abandon physics for the science of the mind.

Some of Britain's more traditional sf writers – Joseph Green, Kenneth Harker, E.C. Tubb – tried to keep up with the new style, with varying degrees of success. (Tubb in particular soon abandoned the attempt and turned to the straightforward space opera of his Dumarest saga, beginning with *The Winds of Gath* (1967)). The writer whose work benefitted most triumphally from the new literary influences was John Brunner. Since the mid-1950s he had been producing hack science fiction and space adventures of varying quality, but in the mid-1960s he started to take the time to experiment. The first result was *The Squares of the City* (1965), which modelled its action on the moves of a chess game, but far more successful was *Stand on Zanzibar* (1968), an examination of the effects of over-population (which had started to impress itself on the political consciousness of the era) using the technique of alternating narrative, stream of consciousness and media reports that John Dos Passos had devised for his monumental *USA* (1930-36). *Stand on Zanzibar* was the most successful blend of sf and modernism that the New Wave produced, earning Brunner a BSFA Award and a

Hugo, and he went on to produce other landmark books such as *The Jagged Orbit* (1969), *The Sheep Look Up* (1972) and especially *The Shockwave Rider* (1975) which has been credited as one of the precursors of cyberpunk.

Michael Moorcock himself showed a similar split in his writing between hack work (colourful fantasies often written in three days to finance *New Worlds* which teetered permanently on the edge of financial collapse, and featuring the flawed but eternal champions, Elric, Corum, Count Brass, who would reappear in different guises in his later work) and fiction that took risks. "Behold the Man" (1966) (later expanded into a novel, 1969) took a modern inadequate, Karl Glogauer, and sent him back in a time machine to witness the crucifixion of Christ. He discovers that the historical Jesus is mentally defective, and finds himself taking on the role of the Messiah, welcoming his own crucifixion as much as any Ballard character might. As is the way with many of Moorcock's characters, Glogauer resurfaced for more self-sacrifice in *Breakfast in the Ruins* (1972), but the most persistent and representative Moorcock hero of this period was Jerry Cornelius (the initials are significant, Moorcock often played with religious symbols). In four novels, *The Final Programme* (1968), *A Cure for Cancer* (1971), *The English Assassin* (1972) and *The Condition of Muzak* (1977), Jerry Cornelius personified all the contradictions, bizarre heroism and selfishness of a messiah figure in the Swinging Sixties. As an icon, travelling in time and able to take on any characteristics demanded of him, Jerry Cornelius was also taken up as a character in stories by other writers in Moorcock's *New Worlds* such as James Sallis, Norman Spinrad and M. John Harrison. Other characters from the Cornelius saga, such as Una Persson and Colonel Pyat, later surfaced in other novels such as the Dancers at the End of Time sequence and the revisionist history of the twentieth century that began with *Byzantium Endures* (1981), though Moorcock's finest work was probably his most restrained and unified, his affectionate portrait of *Mother London* (1982).

Moorcock's most lasting achievement, however, may lie with the editorial genius which fostered a stable of writers who have been among the most distinguished and distinctive voices in science fiction over the last thirty years. These included the Americans Thomas Disch, John Sladek, Pamela Zoline (whose first story, "The Heat Death of the Universe" (1967), was probably the finest and most representative fiction from this whole period), and Norman Spinrad (whose *Bug Jack Barron* (1969) caused questions to be asked in Parliament when it was serialised in shorter form in *New Worlds* in 1967-8). Despite this American involvement, the New Wave imported to the USA by Judith Merrill and Harlan Ellison tended to concentrate on the shock value of iconoclasm rather than the literary experimentalism that was the hallmark of the British New Wave.

Among the British writers that Moorcock encouraged were Hilary Bailey (whose "The Fall of Frenchy Steiner" (1964) was one of the finest of British alternate histories), Barrington Bayley, Michael Butterworth, Graham Charnock, Langdon Jones, James Sallis and the poet D.M. Thomas (whose later fiction, notably *The White Hotel* (1981), contained powerful fantastic imagery). The most significant writers to emerge from this milieu, however, were probably M. John Harrison, Christopher Priest and Josephine Saxton.

Harrison has written horror, science fiction, fantasy and mainstream literature with equal facility and effect. Of this last trio of writers he is the one most closely associated with *New Worlds* and his science fiction, such as "Running Down" (1975) and "Settling the World" (1975), is filled with visions of entropy and decay. His most notable achievement, however, is the importation of a new wave aesthetic with its images of decay and its psycho-sexual insights into fantasy. His first novels about Viriconium, *The Pastel City* (1971) and *A Storm of Wings* (1980) seemed close to conventional heroic fantasy with their stories of an empire in decline and a symbolic quest, but Harrison's dark vision was already undermining the conventions. This was confirmed by *In Viriconium* (1982) and the stories of *Viriconium Nights* (1984) which reveal a land as plastic and tenebrous as anything in Moorcock's multiverse. With two parallel stories, "A Young Man's Journey to Viriconium" (1985) and "Egnaro" (1981), he started exploring the notion of the landscape of the imagination being as real and accessible as anything in this world. It was a direction he confirmed with his latest and finest novel, *The Course of the Heart* (1992).

If Harrison can be seen as Moorcock's natural successor, Christopher Priest is nore like Aldiss's successor, and like Aldiss Priest has an ambivalent and at times antagonistic attitude towards the genre. In essays such as "Outside the Whale" (1980) he would ringingly declare that he was turning his back on a genre he considered already moribund, yet all his fiction, both before and since such declarations, is marked by a clear fascination with the possibilities of the fantastic. His early novels were direct engagements with the notions of science fiction, *Fugue for a Darkening Island* (1972) was a catastrophe novel centring on the influx of African refugees to an unstable Britain after a nuclear war; *Inverted World* (1974) was one of the most inventive novels of post-war British sf with its world turned inside out; *The Space Machine* (1976) paid homage to H.G. Wells as Aldiss had already done (in *The Saliva Tree* (1965)), in this instance providing an ingenious conflation of *The Time Machine* and *The War of the Worlds*. Subsequent novels have been less concerned with the mechanisms of science fiction than with its facility for exploring the mental state of its characters, as in *A Dream of Wessex* (1977), *The Glamour* (1984) and especially in *The Affirmation* (1981), an intense and complex account of mental disintegration in which a character in this world invents a character in the fictional landscape of the Dream Archipelago, but may in his turn be invented by that character from the Dream Archipelago. His most recent novel, *The Prestige* (1995), continues this exploration, using Victorian stage magic as a device for examining the instability of identity through a proliferation of twins and duplicates.

Josephine Saxton, who began to publish at about the same time as Harrison and Priest, has had a far more chequered literary history. Her first three novels, *The Hieros Gamos of Sam and An Smith* (1969), *Vector for Seven* (1970) and *Group Feast* (1971) saw publication only in the USA, despite the fact that her bleak odysseys and complex explorations of personality through mythic archetypes (Jung has been a very powerful influence on her work) had far more in common with what was happening in British sf at the time than American. Her influence in this country was confined to a few powerful and perversely comic short stories until the 1980s, when she was rediscovered by feminist publishers. In her two books that follow her everywoman Jane Saint through a Jungian dreamscape, *The Travails of Jane Saint* (1980, expanded as part of *The Travails of Jane Saint and Other Stories,* 1986) and *Jane Saint and the Backlash* (1989), and particularly her novel of the mental difficulties facing a woman in the contemporary world, *Queen of the States* (1986), Saxton revealed herself to be one of the most effective, idiosyncratic and waspishly funny of all Britain's feminist writers.

Both Priest and Saxton saw their first stories published in *New Worlds'* companion magazine, *Science Fantasy*. *Science Fantasy*, which changed its name briefly to *SF Impulse* before it collapsed, was a home for writers who were not as rigorously experimental as Moorcock's *New Worlds* expected, though this is not to say that it did not make its own impact on the genre, most notably through the work of Keith Roberts. Of all British writers, Roberts is the one whose work shows the deepest and most vivid attachment to the English landscape. His second novel, *Pavane* (1968), was probably his most highly acclaimed. Like much of his work it is a fix-up of related stories which together form a mosaic linked by theme and feel rather than coherent narrative. *Pàvane* is set in a world in which the Spanish Armada succeeded and contemporary England languishes under stultifying Church rule, but although a revolt occurs within the book this drama is not its focus. Roberts' real concern is with the society he creates, the ordinariness of what is to us an extraordinary world: road trains, semaphore signal stations, a girl whose dreams of escape are prompted by smugglers, an inquisitor who rejects the Church in the self-knowledge that he enjoys torturing. *Pavane* is recognised as one of the finest of English alternate histories (despite a coda which reveals it to be concerned with cyclic history) , and it certainly brought out the best in Roberts. "Weinachtsabend" (1972), his most psychologically intense and moving story, follows Katharine Burdekin's *Swastika Night* (1937), Sarban's *The Sound of His Horn* (1952) and Hilary Bailey's "The Fall of Frenchy Steiner" in considering the consequences of Nazi rule, though in his uneasy insights into complicity and self-knowledge "Weinachtsabend" is perhaps the most disturbing of these. Other works, such as *The Chalk Giants* (1974) and *Kiteworld* (1985), if not alternate histories, do involve a sense of cyclic history that is at least as important to the book as is the powerful sense of place. *The Chalk Giants*, arguably his most complex novel, uses the visionary intensity of Paul Nash's surreal landscapes to conjure a picture of history repeating itself as primitive societies and beliefs emerge in the aftermath of nuclear war. The novel also introduced the character that Michael Coney christened the "multi-girl", a protean goddess-woman who provides the catalyst for much of Roberts' work, such as *Grainne* (1987), "Richenda" (1985), and, most vividly, in the character of Kaeti in his two recent collections, *Kaeti and Company* (1986) and *Kaeti on Tour* (1992).

Again and again, Roberts' fiction turns to the English landscape, Purbeck and Corfe Castle loom particularly large in his imagination, and he evokes a spirit of place with genuine fluency and affect. Of his contemporaries, only Richard Cowper comes close to matching this. In novels and stories such as *The Twilight of Briareus* (1974), "The Custodians" (1975) and "The Tithonian Factor" (1983) he presents an image of the landscape, often damaged or disrupted in some way, which reflects the drama in which his protagonists are trapped. This is best demonstrated by his sequence of novels, *The Road to Corlay* (1978), *A Dream of Kinship* (1981) and *A Tapestry of Time* (1982), which explore the consequences of a messiah figure emerging in a drowned England (a landscape which parallels the dreamscape of Priest's *A Dream of Wessex*).

If this selection of writers suggests that British sf at this time was exclusively the domain of psychological exploration and consciously literary effect, it is only necessary to mention the variety of authors from the astronomer Fred Hoyle (*The Black Cloud* (1957)) to Edmund Cooper (*Sea-Horse in the Sky* (1969), *The Cloud Walker* (1973)) who were turning out hard science fiction and fantastic adventures with the best of them. At the same time, Northern Ireland gave us James White and Bob Shaw. White, in novels like *The Dream Millenium* (1974) and especially the Sector General stories such as *Hospital Station* (1962) and *Star Surgeon* (1963), was proving that there was still vigour and life to be found in the most traditional tropes and devices of science fiction, from time travel to interstellar adventure. After Clarke, Shaw comes the closest any British writer has got to the core of genre science fiction. His invention of slow glass in his Hugo-winning "Light of Other Days" (1966) was the first truly new notion to come out of science fiction for many years. In his best work, *The Palace of Eternity* (1969) which ventures into the afterlife, *A Wreath of Stars* (1976) in which an antineutrino "Earth" is discovered within our own, *Orbitsville* (1975) which takes us inside a Dyson sphere, and *The Ragged Astronauts* (1986) which plausibly tells of a journey between planets by balloon, he shows a superb ability to manipulate sf devices for dramatic effect coupled with a concern for character which marks him out as a distinctively British writer.

The 1960s was an era in which science fiction discovered the literary mainstream, but the traffic was two-way. Lawrence Durrell, who had already played with notions of time in his *Alexandria Quartet* (1957-60), would employ robots and artificial intelligence in *Tunc* (1968) and its sequel, *Numi uam* (1970). Angus Wilson used a near-future setting for his satirical look at British neofascism, *The Old Men at the Zoo* (1961). Anthony Burgess used science fiction as the basis for his satirical dystopia, *A Clockwork Orange* (1962), and would venture into the genre again in such books as *1985* (1978) and *The End of the World News* (1983). Naomi Mitchison, who has flirted constantly with the fantastic throughout her long career, wrote among others a post-modern take on the Arthurian cycle in *To the Chapel Perilous* (1955) as well as her famous work of feminist science fiction, *Memoirs of a Spacewoman* (1962). If these books represent one end of a spectrum, the other is provided by television which, at the time, was showing *Dr Who*, *The Avengers*, *The Prisoner* and *Star Trek* among others, all programmes which were instrumental in turning the fantastic into an accepted part of British popular culture.

Chapter Five

Becoming Invisible

THE SIXTIES ENDED not with a bang but a whimper. Harold Wilson's Labour Government was replaced by the Conservative Government of Edward Heath in 1970, but persistent industrial unrest, culminating in the three-day-week, swept Wilson back into power in 1974. This new Labour Government would be plagued by strikes too, including the notorious Winter of Discontent which brought Britain closer to a General Strike than at any time since 1926. Sixties dreams of affluence and full employment were shattered by a new reality of rampant inflation and massive debt. If there was not quite a retreat to the conformity of the Fifties, there was at least an air of retrenchment and constraint. The expansive optimism of the Sixties was over, and with it the colour and experiment it engendered. Despite artificial flourishes (such as the phenomenon of Glam Rock) the arts would follow a very traditional formula in these years. (In America, for example, the most significant new writer to emerge in science fiction at this time was John Varley, who turned his back on the brief flourish of the American New Wave in favour of Heinleinesque story telling.) But even the traditional was no longer safe; critics in America, misinterpreting the first, very self-conscious efforts of postmodern fiction, were already proclaiming the death of the novel.

It was in such an atmosphere that *New Worlds* bowed to the inevitable. For years its existence had been, at best, hand to mouth and now the magazine folded. The name lived on through the Seventies as a paperback anthology, *New Worlds Quarterly* (though it was anything but, seeing only 10 issues between 1971 and 1976), under the editorship, variously, of Michael Moorcock, Hilary Bailey and Charles Platt. Its only rival as an outlet for short fiction in this country was the much more traditional *New Writings in Science Fiction*, another original anthology series which had been created by E.J. Carnell when he gave up the editorship of *New Worlds*. *New Writings*, edited first by Carnell then by Kenneth Bulmer, just survived the Seventies, its last issue, 30, appearing in 1978.

Ironically, this was a time when science fiction was going through one of its periodic booms, fuelled at least in part by the interest aroused by programmes such as *Dr Who* and *Star Trek* on television. A variety of magazines appeared, attempting to exploit this gap in the market, but most lasted no more than an issue or two. The most successful, *Science Fiction Monthly*, backed by the publisher New English Library, was largely responsible for a massive influx of new attendees at the annual British Easter Science Fiction Convention in the mid-Seventies, demonstrating the growth of interest in science fiction at the time; but even so it failed to find a sustainable market and the magazine folded after two years.

Up to this point it had been a peculiarity of science fiction that new writers would find their feet writing short stories before moving on to novels, perhaps because in science fiction the ideas carry as much weight as the writing and while writing skills can be learned at longer length, ideas are best worked out in short fiction before they are strong enough to sustain a novel. With the decline in outlets for new short fiction, therefore, there was a consequent decline in new writers. Throughout the Seventies, in fact, there was a feeling of marking time, and even the massive impact of films like *Star Wars* and the original radio dramatisation of *The Hitch Hiker's Guide to the Galaxy* took time to translate into a growth in new writers. Indeed, it was not until the launch of another magazine, *Interzone*, that the groundwork was laid for the influx of new writers that has been a feature of the late-Eighties and early-Nineties.

It is no surprise that most of the writers who did emerge during the Seventies and early Eighties had begun their careers in the final moments of the new wave. Indeed, the early work of writers such as Robert Holdstock, Garry Kilworth and Christopher Evans owes a considerable debt to writers such as Christopher Priest and M. John Harrison. Holdstock's early novels, for instance, *Eye Among the Blind* (1976) and *Earthwind* (1977) used traditional science fictional devices, alien worlds and beings, but the dense writing style loaded these devices with images of loss, mutilation and defeat. Running through his work, however, there was a strong theme of ritual and tradition, a closeness to the soil, that came out in stories such as "Ash, Ash" (1974) and "Earth and Stone" (1980). This tendency, an interest not in myth itself but in the origin of myth, finally came out in the story "Mythago Wood" (1981, expanded as a novel 1984) and its sequels, *Lavondyss* (1988), *The Bone Forest* (1991) and *The Hollowing* (1993). These stories take as their premise the notion that a stand of primordial woodland survives in England in which are to be found the "myth imagoes" which are the irreducible and generally violent forms of our most basic myths. Hovering somewhere in the hinterland between fantasy, science fiction and horror, these stories have been among the most original and intensely worked-out examples of British fantastic literature of recent years.

Christopher Evans' first novel, *Capella's Golden Eyes* (1980), had the same very literary but slightly uneasy approach to traditional science fiction devices as Holdstock's *Eye Among the Blind*. With *In Limbo* (1985), a chill study of alienation and one of his best works, he seemed to be even more firmly in the *New Worlds*, New Wave camp. Evans is not, however, a prolific writer, and the few books that have appeared over the years have tended to drift in a variety of directions, from the baroque fantasy of *Chimeras* (1992) to alternate history with his BSFA Award-winning *Aztec Century* (1994). He has been a skilful and effective writer in each of these formats, but he has made none his own.

Garry Kilworth is similarly restless, but with a much greater output to his credit he has been able to make more of a mark on the genre. His early novels, *In Solitary* (1977) and *The Night of Kadar* (1978), were very much in the mode of his contemporaries, using genre materials such as alien worlds and alien beings, but with a distanced feel and a fascination with defeat that show the legacy of the New Wave. But Kilworth is a much better and more persistent short story writer than any of his contemporaries, which has allowed him to experiment in a wide range of styles, and this has fed through into his novels. His work has included poetry (*Tree Messiah* (1985)), mainstream fiction (*Witchwater Country* (1986)), animal fantasy (*Hunter's Moon* (1989)), surreal fiction ("Hogfoot Right and Bird Hands" (1987)) and horror (*Angel* (1993)). Most of this has been highly successful, though his best work to date is probably science fiction, in particular *Cloudrock* (1988) with its story of brother pitted against brother in a curiously isolated landscape and *Abandonati* (1988) which tells of the struggle for existence in a desolate, abandoned London.

The most dramatic debut in British science fiction during this period, however, probably belongs to Ian Watson. His first novel, *The Embedding* (1973), was one of the most complex and enthralling books of the time, marrying images of entropy with an awareness of modern philosophy which allowed him to propose language as a key to transcendence. He followed that with equally pyrotechnic novels, *The Jonah Kit* (1975) which involved cetacean intelligence and *The Martian Inca* (1977) in which Martian dust triggered transcendence. The richness and vigour of the ideas that fuelled these first three books could not be sustained, but later stories such as *The Gardens of Delight* (1980), a fantasy constructed around the Hieronymous Bosch triptych, the Black Current trilogy (*The Book of the River* (1984), *The Book of the Stars* (1985) and *The Book of Being* (1985)) about a conflict between metaphysical entities in a world split by an apparently sentient river, "Stalin's Teardrops" (1990) with its postmodern equation of landscape and imagination and *Lucky's Harvest* (1993) and its sequel *The Fallen Moon* (1994) which project the images and incidents of Finnish legend onto a science fiction scenario, all demonstrate that he can be one of the most original and interesting writers in British sf today.

There is something distinctly British in the attitudes and subject matter of all four of these writers, but the author who emerged in this country during the Seventies to enjoy far and away the most popular success does not fit into this mould at all. In fact, most of Tanith Lee's books have been published first in America, and a number of them have never seen British publication. Her work has varied between the outright science fiction of *Silver Metal Lover* (1981) and the outright heroic fantasy of *The Birthgrave* (1975), but she has become increasingly a decadent writer, using images of male violence and female vampirism, replete with sexuality, to produce tales of female independence, cruelty and sexual complicity. In *Vivia* (1995), for instance, her female central character, the sole survivor of a plague, endures by surrendering her being to a dark god and becoming a vampire in the process. She is later captured by a rival lord (Lee's novels frequently feature images of imprisonment and slavery) and held as his mistress and a participant in his magical/sexual experiments, while a harem of young girls is supplied for her own tastes. Other writers of this generation, notably Steve Gallagher in *Valley of Lights* (1987), Kim Newman in *Anno Dracula* (1992) and Brian Stableford in *Empire of Fear* (1988), have revived the vampire as a resonant image of anxiety, alienation and, of course, sexual fear heightened by the AIDS epidemic. Stableford also, in the anthologies he has compiled for Dedalus, has done much to rediscover decadence as a literary form, but no other contemporary writer has brought together decadence and vampirism as wholeheartedly as Tanith Lee.

Lee's strong female characters, who typically have to contend with the cruel usage of men, have at times caused her to be included with writers of feminist science fiction. Indeed, one of her collections of short stories was published by The Women's Press, a publishing house which did much to raise the awareness of feminist science fiction in this country during the 1980s by publishing such writers as Rhoda Lerman (*The Book of the Night* (1984)), Jane Palmer (*The Planet Dweller* (1985) and *The Watcher* (1986)), Margaret Elphinstone (*The Incomer* (1987) and *A Sparrow's Flight* (1989)) and Sue Thomas (*Correspondence*, 1991). The most impressive feminist voices in science fiction in this country, though in very different ways, were probably Lisa Tuttle, Doris Lessing, Mary Gentle and Gwyneth Jones.

Lisa Tuttle, an American who has been resident in Britain since 1980, has turned again and again to consider the roles women play, perhaps most notably in the novel *Lost Futures*

(1992) in which her heroine finds herself moving between alternative realities and in the collection *Memories of the Body: Tales of Desire and Transformation* (1992). Though she has written science fiction effectively, most of her best work has tended towards a contemporary, urban horror. Doris Lessing, who had already established herself as one of the most powerful voices in feminism with novels such as *The Golden Notebook* (1962) and *The Four-Gated City* (1969), had often incorporated fantastic or futuristic elements into her work. When she moved most boldly into the genre she chose to abandon contemporary Earth other than as a target for satire, writing what she chose to call "space fiction". Her Canopus in Argos sequence (*Shikasta* (1979), *The Marriage Between Zones Three, Four, and Five* (1980), *The Sirian Experiments* (1981), *The Making of the Representative for Planet 8* (1982) and *The Sentimental Agents in the Volyen Empire* (1983)) uses elements of Eastern metaphysics in its examination of sexual and political clashes. Mary Gentle has chosen yet a third route. The novels that first brought her to general notice, *Golden Witchbreed* (1983) and *Ancient Light* (1987), were planetary adventures which draw an uneasy parallel between her colonised planet Orthe and our own third world. Her more recent work, however, has been much more complex and darker still, drawing on elements of hermetic philosophy in the story of White Crow an ambivalent heroine who, rather like Keith Roberts' Kaeti, reappears in very different settings. In *Rats and Gargoyles* (1990) it is an alternate late-medieval Britain, in *The Architecture of Desire* (1991) an alternate early-modern, Cromwellian Britain, and in *Left to Her Own Devices* (1994) an alternate contemporary Britain. In each of her works the competent yet fallible heroine presents a tacit feminist message.

There is little tacit about the works of Gwyneth Jones. Her rich and allusive novels, which take as their main subject human communication or, rather, our inability to communicate, impel the reader into worlds that are never explained until the reader has come to understand them for herself through the eyes of Jones' characters. Though she was already an established writer of fantasy and science fiction for children, it was her first novel for adults, *Divine Endurance* (1984), which brought her to popular attention. The innocent female android, whose journey through a vividly realised post-apocalyptic South East Asia leaves civil war in her wake, also has her analogue in Jones's next two novels. Both *Escape Plans* (1986) and *Kairos* (1988), along with the sequel to *Divine Endurance, Flowerdust* (1993), place their innocent female protagonist as the trigger in a tale of degeneration and redemption. *White Queen* (1991) and *North Wind* (1994), in contrast, take us beyond such questions of sex since the humans are unable to recognise the sex of the Aleutian aliens who arrive to colonise Earth, and indeed go on to mutilate themselves to approximate the physical characteristics of the aliens. These novels provide a sexual recasting on the familiar story of European colonisation in the third world.

It is worth noticing that Jones uses pronouns to confuse and obscure sexual identity in these novels in much the same way that Storm Constantine does in her novels of sex and androgyny in highly coloured science fictional settings, most notably the Wraeththu trilogy, *The Enchantments of Flesh and Spirit* (1987), *The Bewitchments of Love and Hate* (1988) and *The Fulfilments of Fate and Desire* (1989). More recently, Constantine's novels such as *Hermetech* (1991) and *Sign for the Sacred* (1993) have taken this exoticism towards a sexual decadence reminiscent of Tanith Lee.

If feminism was one of the strong currents running through British science fiction and fantasy in the 1980s, the other was instigated by the appearance, in 1982, of a new British sf magazine, *Interzone*, edited initially by a collective of writers and fans but since 1988 solely by David Pringle. Britain, for so long without a regular market for short fiction, was on the verge of a sudden tidal wave of short stories. In its early issues in particular, *Interzone* was frequently criticised for attempting too slavishly to revive the style and tone of Moorcock's *New Worlds* (an image that regular contributions from Ballard, Aldiss, M. John Harrison, Barrington Bayley and Moorcock himself did little to dispel). Nevertheless, it did start to introduce new writers such as Eric Brown, Paul J. McAuley and Stephen Baxter, and in its wake came original anthologies (*Other Edens* edited by Christopher Evans and Robert Holdstock, *Zenith* edited by David Garnett, and most recently a revived *New Worlds* also edited by Garnett) and semi-professional magazines to an extent that Britain had not seen before.

In 1979 the Labour Government of James Callaghan, bedevilled by strikes and economic disarray, had been swept from power by the Conservatives under Margaret Thatcher. The new government brought in harsh economic measures and centralised controls which, like the attacks on trade union membership and the short-lived poll tax, were seen as restricting individual freedom, hence the number of failed utopias, feminist or otherwise, which appeared at this time, while the national mood of ineffectual dismay may have accounted in part for the downbeat nature of the stories in early issues of *Interzone*. At the same time there were periods of economic boom which created a climate in which these new fiction outlets could develop, though the cycles of economic decline which alternated with the boom may explain why most of the outlets were short-lived. Of the original anthology series, the longest lived was the revived *New Worlds* which lasted four issues; while the semi-professional magazines have tended to be sporadic and the only one which has survived long enough and with an editorial policy adventurous enough to challenge *Interzone* has been *Back Brain Recluse* (latterly known as *BBR*) edited by Chris Reed. Nevertheless, the very existence of new markets has resulted in an upsurge in British science fiction and fantasy during the 1980s and 90s.

One of the first and most impressive talents to emerge from this milieu was the Canadian writer Geoff Ryman, who has been resident in Britain since 1973. His first published story was in *New Worlds* in 1976 ("The Diary of the Translator"), but it was in *Interzone* with "The Unconquered Country" (1984, revised as a novel 1986) and "Love Sickness" (1987, revised as the novel *The Child Garden*, 1988), that his ability to use science fiction to serious effect became obvious. *The Unconquered Country* uses bizarre fantasy and sf devices, houses with legs, women selling their wombs to grow weapons, to create a haunting image of Cambodia devastated by war. The agony transfixed at the heart of *The Child Garden* is more immediate, the agony of social and sexual identity in a transfigured London where people photosynthesise and genetically mutated viruses are used to implant knowledge, science fictional devices again expressing the alienation of the individual up against the impersonal authority of the state. This sense of human individuality being stamped upon by those in power is explicit in his short story, "O Happy Day" (1985), in which homosexuals are confined in a concentration camp. His most personal and most delicately wrought novel, however, is *Was...* (1992), in which the private agonies of the real girl who inspired L. Frank Baum's *The Wonderful Wizard of Oz* (1900) resonate with the story of the making of the film, the story of an actor dying of AIDS and the story of the real Dorothy dying after a lifetime in a mental institution.

Among the other writers of what might be called the *Interzone* generation (though not all of them first appeared in the magazine and some have not been published there), most are still so close to the start of their careers that it is difficult to be sure which way their work will develop. Most, however, have made a point of incorporating very traditional science fictional motifs into their work. Eric Brown's stories, collected in *The Time Lapsed Man* (1990) as well as novels such as *Meridian Days* (1992) and *Engineman* (1994), seem to show mostly the influence of Michael Coney in his artists, or would-be artists, washed up on the shores of alien worlds. Keith Brooke has also set his novels, *Expatria* (1991) and *Expatria Incorporated* (1992), on alien planets, as have Alison Sinclair with her tale of guilt and lost technologies, *Legacies* (1995), and Anne Gay with her highly coloured and sometimes over-wrought novels of colony worlds, *Dancing on the Volcano* (1993) and *To Bathe in Lightning* (1995). David Wingrove envisages a world-encompassing future Chinese empire in his ongoing series *Chung Kuo* which began with *The Middle Kingdom* (1989). Simon Ings seems to have taken a step beyond cyberpunk in *Hot Head* (1992) and *Hotwire* (1995), though he comes closer to M. John Harrison in *City of the Iron Fish* (1994), and Peter Hamilton has chosen that most British of scenarios with a story of ecological disaster against which he plays out an adventure story with cyberpunk trappings in *Mindstar Rising* (1993). Curiously, although both *Interzone* and *BBR* have played host to leading American cyberpunk writers such as Bruce Sterling, Richard Kadrey and Paul Di Filippo, other than a few short stories that echo the American model too closely, British writers have generally not taken up cyberpunk with much enthusiasm. One exception is Jeff Noon, whose debut novel, *Vurt* (1993), paints a gripping portrait of a near-future Manchester in which the creations of dream, drugs and virtual reality are infecting the real world; another recent debut, *Only Forward* (1994) by Michael Marshall Smith, similarly invokes dream as the instigation for this curious, balkanised dystopia. In the main, though, Britain's younger writers seem much more ready to follow an older tradition of science fiction.

Paul J. McAuley, for instance, evokes echoes of Arthur C. Clarke especially in *Eternal Light* (1991), the pyrotechnic conclusion to his early trio of space operas which climaxes with a transcendental voyage to the heart of the universe. In *Red Dust* (1993) he turned to Mars. McAuley is not the only British writer to add to the recent welter of novels about Mars, both Ian McDonald and Colin Greenland have ventured to the planet also, but he was the only one who has come close to portraying the Mars known to scientific observation rather than the Mars invented by science fiction of the past. Even so, his story twists the normal pattern by portraying the red planet as dominated by Chinese communism. McAuley is one of the few trained scientists to make a mark on post-war British sf (others include Fred Hoyle and Brian Stableford, whose training in biology lies behind his caustic stories of genetic research collected in *Sexual Chemistry* (1991)). It is curious that each of these has been attracted to the unscientific form of alternate history (Hoyle with *October the First is Too Late* (1966) and Stableford with *Empire of Fear* (1988)) and McAuley also has followed the pattern with his tale of a very different Renaissance Italy, *Pasquale's Angel* (1994).

Like Tanith Lee before him, Ian McDonald is another British writer whose initial success came in America; in fact he had a collection of short stories, *Empire Dreams* (1988), and a novel, *Desolation Road* (1988), published before his work made anything but a cursory appearance in this country. Since then, however, he has become one of the most highly acclaimed of his generation of writers. Like so many others, McDonald has put the apparatus of science fiction at the heart of his fiction, but in his case there is a knowing reference to the authors who supplied his tropes and gestures. *Desolation Road*, a long and often plotless account of a small town on Mars and the curious collection of misfits and wanderers who gather there, revisits the Mars of Ray Bradbury rather than NASA surveys but its narrative manner, shifting focus from one character to another over an extended time period, with the location more than any individual binding the book together, and the almost magical appearance of some of the characters, is reminiscent more of *One Hundred Years of Solitude* (1967) by Gabriel Garcia Marquez. In other work, such as *Hearts, Hands and Voices* (1992), his model seems to be Geoff Ryman. Such echoes do not betoken any lack of originality in his work, they are put to his own ends; rather they recognise science fiction as a tradition that can now be appropriated. This sense of science fiction's past, often in the form of ironic self-awareness as in the work of Iain M. Banks and Colin Greenland, has become a common feature of contemporary British science fiction. This self-conscious use of form does not limit the import of what is being written, however, and McDonald, who is resident in Northern Ireland, has included perceptive comment on Irish identity and religious conflict in much of his fiction, most notably *King of Morning, Queen of Day* (1991), a fantasy novel expanded from a 1985 short story.

If younger British writers were operating almost exclusively within the heartland of the genre, an older generation was looking towards the mainstream. Brian Aldiss (*Forgotten Life* (1988)), J.G. Ballard (*Empire of the Sun* (1984)), M. John Harrison (*Climbers* (1989)) and Christopher Priest (*The Quiet Woman* (1990)) all wrote mainstream novels during the 1980s, and started to receive the sort of critical attention they had tended to miss out on as genre writers. At the same time a number of writers from outside the genre were turning more and more to the possibilities of science fiction. Writers as varied as Peter Ackroyd (*Hawksmoor* (1985)), Martin Amis (*Einstein's Monsters* (1987) and *Time's Arrow* (1991)), Julian Barnes (*Staring at the Sun* (1986)), John Fowles (*Mantissa* (1982) and *A Maggot* (1985)), P.D. James (*The Children of Men* (1992)), Ian McEwan (*The Child in Time* (1987)), Salman Rushdie (*Grimus* (1975) and *Midnight's Children* (1980)), Paul Theroux (*O-Zone* (1986)) and E.P. Thompson (*The Sykaos Papers* (1988)) all used science fictional or fantastic devices in their work, with varying degrees of success. Even thriller writers were employing alternate history scenarios, usually ones in which Germany won the Second World War, as in *SS-GB* (1978) by Len Deighton and *Fatherland* (1992) by Robert Harris. (The novels by James, Theroux and Thompson in particular are stunning examples of bad work by people with little feel for or interest in the genre they are plundering.) What was happening, in effect, was that the barriers which had once divided science fiction from the mainstream were becoming blurred, with writers dipping in and out of the fantastic as their imaginations dictated.

One of the things which lay behind this growing invisibility of the ghetto walls was the influx of postmodern fiction which was being taken up by more and more writers. Just as fantasy had long been a favourite tool of satirists (one notable recent example being Andrew Sinclair's extraordinarily fierce three-volume attack on the post-war history of Britain in *Gog* (1967), *Magog* (1972) and *King Ludd* (1988)), so science fiction was picked up by postmodernists, its obvious fictionality suiting their agenda of breaking down the perceived barriers between fiction, reality, reader and text. Two British writers in particular have explored the joint possibilities of postmodernism and the fantastic to create works of astonishing vigour and originality.

Alasdair Gray is a Scottish artist whose first novel, *Lanark* (1981), was one of the landmark books of the decade, defying genre categorisation (at one point he incorporates into the book a long list of books which influenced its writing, many of them overtly science fictional, including work by his fellow Glaswegian Chris Boyce). *Lanark* tells the story of the life and death of a struggling artist, Duncan Thaw, in contemporary Scotland, a story which contains both humour and a heartfelt argument for the Scottish Nationalist cause. However, this apparent *roman à clef* is sandwiched between the story of Duncan, now renamed Lanark, in an afterlife known as Unthank (the idiosyncratic structure of the book is such that the Prologue occurs after 100 pages of text). Lanark's odyssey through Unthank goes on to reveal this afterlife to be the text of the novel *Lanark*. Since this breathtaking debut Gray has never quite been able to attain the same energy and invention, though he has come close in novels which also contain a strong fantastic element, notably his metaphysical fantasy, *1982, Janine*

41

(1984), his sharp reworking of the Frankenstein theme in *Poor Things* (1992) and his ironically exuberant Scottish utopia, *A History Maker* (1994).

Angela Carter who, among other things, edited anthologies of and translated fairy stories, was always ready to use the fantastic in her fiction. Sometimes her work came close to science fiction in its settings and imagery, as when she parodied social stratification in a post-holocaust England in *Heroes and Villains* (1969) or when she embarked on a picaresque journey across an America on the point of the holocaust in *The Passion of New Eve* (1977), but these were also fantasies of sexual awakening and her work was often at its best when she could tinge the real with the irrational and sexual, as in *The Magic Toyshop* (1967) or *The Infernal Desire Machines of Doctor Hoffman* (1972). In her finest work, such as her violent and sexual reworkings of traditional fairy stories collected in *The Bloody Chamber* (1979) and her vivid and richly symbolic novel of a circus performer who had genuine wings, *Nights at the Circus* (1984), her use of folk tales with their happy acceptance of outbreaks of the irrational to illuminate strongly feminist fictions made her work closer to the Latin American magic realists than any of her British contemporaries.

Other British writers, though, such as Robert Irwin (*The Limits of Vision* (1986), *The Arabian Nightmare* (1983 revised 1987), and *Exquisite Corpse* (1995), have come close to this description, while a *sui generis* writer such as Iain Sinclair, whose prose-poem *Lud Heat* (1975) was an inspiration for Ackroyd's *Hawksmoor*, seems to occupy some peculiar, lunatic ground where magic realism and postmodernism, shamanism and obsession, collide in such curious forms of fantasy as *White Chappell, Scarlet Tracings* (1987) and *Radon Daughters* (1994).

Away from such oddities, fantasy has enjoyed something of a revival over recent years. This is not just because of the growing interest in the form from the mainstream, although such reworkings of British popular myth as *Merlin* (1978) by Robert Nye certainly helped. One of the prime causes was certainly the emergence of Tolkien's *The Lord of the Rings* as a cult classic during the mid-Sixties which prompted a flood of imitations on both sides of the Atlantic. The most successful in this country has been David Gemmell who has written a series of muscular fantasy adventures such as the Drenai Saga (*Legend* (1984), *The King Beyond the Gate* (1985), *Waylander* (1986) and *Quest for Lost Heroes* (1990)) and his fantasy reworkings of the story of Alexander the Great, *Lion of Macedon* (1990) and *Dark Prince* (1991). Such forms of heroic fantasy continue to be written in great number, though most have a more romantic edge than Gemmell's work, as in *Moths to a Flame* (1995) by Sarah Ash, or they edge away from straight fantasy. Some merge fantasy with science fictional motifs, as *Albion* (1991) and *The World* (1992) by John Grant (Paul Barnett) who has also written fantasy such as the Lone Wolf series derived from role-playing games with Joe Dever, and science fiction, such as *Earthdoom!* (1987) with David Langford. Others combine fantasy with historical fiction, particularly in such retellings of the Arthur story as by Mary Stewart (*The Crystal Cave* (1970), *The Hollow Hills* (1973) and *The Last Enchantment* (1979)) or Fay Sampson's feminist approach (*Wise Woman's Telling* (1989), *White Nun's Telling* (1989), *Black Smith's Telling* (1990), *Taliesin's Telling* (1991) and *Herself* (1992)).

Before embarking on this quintet, Sampson was best known as a writer of children's fantasy, another form of the genre which has achieved notable quality. Two of the finest British exponents over recent years have been Alan Garner and Diana Wynne Jones. Garner's first novels, *The Weirdstone of Brisingamen* (1960) and *The Moon of Gomrath* (1963), were pure fantasy, tying in aspects of the legend of King Arthur with the folklore of his native Alderley Edge in Cheshire. Since then, however, his work has gradually darkened through the alternate world quest of *Elidor* (1965) and the bitter sexual frustration and violent re-enactment of Welsh myth in *The Owl Service* (1967) to the grim, jagged movements through time of perhaps his best but most elliptical novel *Red Shift* (1973). Diana Wynne Jones has an altogether lighter tone; practically all her novels are comedies, though this disguises some often disturbing perceptions about identity, adulthood and freedom. A prolific writer, her finest works include her satirical view of local government and writer's block, *Archer's Goon* (1984), her most overtly science fictional novel about the breakdown of reality, *A Tale of Time City* (1987), and her haunting retelling of the legend of Tam Lin in *Fire and Hemlock* (1985). If science fiction for children has fared less well it is no fault of John Christopher, who has transformed his disaster novels for adults into equally successful disaster novels for children, notably his Tripods sequence, *The White Mountains* (1967), *The City of Gold and Lead* (1967), *The Pool of Fire* (1968) and a belated prequel, *When the Tripods Came* (1988).

However, the forms of fantasy which have been most successful of late have been comedy and what has become known as "dark fantasy". Before 1978 comic fantasy or science fiction was rare, largely because it depended on a knowledge of the genre for its effect which meant there was no ready audience outside the limited number of sf fans. By the late 1970s, however, *Star Trek* and *Dr Who*, *Star Wars* and *Close Encounters of the Third Kind* had created a much wider awareness of science fiction even among non-readers of the genre, and when the radio series *The Hitch Hiker's Guide to the Galaxy* began on the BBC in 1978 it acquired a rapid and unexpected cult following. Douglas Adams, who created the series, followed it up with books, a TV series, even a computer game. Sf comedy as we know it was born.

Adams' subsequent work, *Dirk Gently's Holistic Detective Agency* (1987) and *The Long Dark Tea-Time of the Soul* (1988), never quite repeated the success he found in endless re-cyclings of *The Hitch Hiker's Guide*, and as a genre humorist he was soon to be overtaken by Terry Pratchett. Pratchett had already poked gentle fun at the genre in books such as *The Dark Side of the Sun* (1976) but it was his creation of the Discworld in *The Colour of Magic* (1983) that transformed him into one of the most successful writers in the genre, each new volume in the ongoing saga (most recently, *Interesting Times* (1994)) has propelled him directly to the top of the bestseller lists. His success has, of course, created an opportunity for other humorists, from Robert Rankin (*The Most Amazing Man Who Ever Lived* (1995)), to Tom Holt (*Here Comes the Sun* (1993) and *Faust Among Equals* (1994)), to John Brosnan (*Damned and Fancy* (1995)) though few actually match his clever pastiche of subjects we know well but not too well, from Shakespeare (*Wyrd Sisters* (1988)) to ancient Egypt (*Pyramids* (1989)).

Dark fantasy, on the other hand, is a crossover between fantasy and horror, a form that has become increasingly popular over the last few years. It seems to apply to any form of horror which does not go into outright Lovecraftian grotesquery or the contemporary urban serial killer format. It is a term that is used equally for the textured psychological hauntings of Graham Joyce's *Dark Sister* (1992) and *House of Lost Dreams* (1993), and for Stephen Marley's magical adventure stories set in Ancient China, *Mortal Mask* (1991) and *Shadow Sisters* (1992). As for straight horror, despite works by Ramsey Campbell, James Herbert, Stephen Gallagher and Kim Newman, it has tended to follow the pattern set by Stephen King with little overtly supernatural or fantastic about it.

One writer whose first novel seemed to predicate a place among contemporary horror writers has confounded that expectation by producing some of the most successful genre science fiction of the decade. Iain Banks (who uses the form Iain M. Banks for his overtly science fictional work) began his career with one of the most controversial novels of the 1980s, *The Wasp Factory* (1984), a gripping, horrific tale of murder and psychological damage. Even this supposedly mainstream work had surreal and fantastical overtones which became more and more explicit in his subsequent books until with *Consider Phlebas* (1987) he produced a full-blown space opera. This initiated a series of novels on a vast scale (epic size is one of the consistent features in Banks' science fiction, from the space ships as large as cities to the monumental, Gormenghast-like palace of *Feersum Endjinn* (1994)) about a far future space-going civilisation known as the Culture. The Culture novels are unusual for such galaxy-spanning tales for featuring a time of plenty when there is no Empire, in fact the Culture seems to be an effective anarchy, reflecting Banks' pronounced left-wing sympathies. At the same time, each novel looks at the Culture from a perspective of questioning or antagonism, whether the central character is the mercenary at war with the Culture in *Consider Phlebas* or the dilettante being used by it in *Player of Games* (1988). Although his more recent science fiction novels, *Against a Dark Background* (1993) and *Feersum Endjinn*, are not part of the Culture sequence, they have the same epic scale and the same edgy fascination with violence. *Against a Dark Background* follows a female mercenary as she tries to escape the religious cult that is hunting her, while *Feersum Endjinn* follows four disparate characters as they make their separate ways through the interstices of a vast palace on missions that collide in mysterious subversion.

This presentation of science fiction as wide-screen adventure is something that has been taken up by other contemporary British writers, the most significant of whom is Colin Greenland. After a number of narrow, stylish but essentially pallid fantasies, the most interesting of which was the first, *Daybreak on a Different Mountain* (1984), he undertook a sudden change of pace and produced *Take Back Plenty* (1990), a bold, fast-paced, old-fashioned space adventure which, in one fell swoop, propelled him to the front rank of British science fiction. A sequel, *Seasons of Plenty* (1995) continues the adventure, while the intervening novel, *Harm's Way* (1993), sets off in another bright and vivid direction with a story of Victorian spacefarers taking sailing ships to Mars. This knowing (at times too knowing) employment of genre cliches and effects is one of the most consistent features of contemporary British science fiction. It is a manner exemplified by Stephen Baxter's most recent novel. In novels such as *Raft* (1991) and *Flux* (1994) he has established himself as one of the few British writers working consistently within the hard sf field, but *The Time Ships* (1995) reveals a more thorough working out of the history of the genre. Starting as a straight sequel to *The Time Machine* by H.G. Wells, he takes the reader on an exhilarating ride through just about every aspect of Wells's science fiction and in so doing brings the history of the genre in Britain round full circle.

Epilogue

IT IS NOW SOME 180 years since a group of people sat down to tell each other ghost stories beside Lake Geneva, and the idea for *Frankenstein* was born. At the time it seemed like another in the long tradition of British fantastic literature, imbued with the fashionably dark atmosphere of the Gothic and decorated with notions taken from the philosophical and scientific thought of the day. In retrospect it seems more than that: a turning point that shifted Gothic fantasy onto a new course, a course that would lead to modern science fiction.

A hundred years ago, a young writer published his first, short novel, *The Time Machine*. Over the next half-century he would follow it with a string of works which established the tone and ninety per cent of the subject matter of science fiction ever since.

These are the key milestones in the history of British science fiction. In this essay I have tried to show that, if Britain wasn't alone in giving science fiction to the world, it was one of the most important generators of the genre. More than that, I have tried to suggest that it has developed from those early forebears in a way that is distinctively its own. Until very recently, science fiction in America, for instance, seems to have been a very isolated literature, largely unaffected by other literary movements around it. In contrast, science fiction in Britain has developed in a surprisingly close relationship with both the long tradition of British fantastic writing (such that it is often difficult, if not impossible, to draw a clear distinction between fantasy and science fiction and certain themes, such as the Arthurian Cycle, continue to form a part of our literature, explicit and implicit, across all genre boundaries) and with the literary mainstream. Perhaps because the fantastic has such an honourable place in the British literary tradition, serious and popular writers from Charles Dickens to Martin Amis have always shown a readiness to move into genre territory as the spirit takes them.

This doesn't mean that science fiction in this country has always been critically respectable. Even today it is probably harder to get a space adventure or a sword and sorcery novel reviewed seriously in the general press than it is just about any other literary form except pornography. But the borders of the genre are wider and less clearly defined than they might otherwise be: science fiction, fantasy, horror, the mainstream, crime fiction, children's literature all merge into each other and cross-fertilise. The result has been the health and variety of British fantastic literature which I have tried to celebrate in this short book.

45

Bibliography

ALDISS, Brian with David Wingrove, *Trillion Year Spree*, Paladin, 1988

ALLEN, Virginia, "Ethos and Marginalization in the Henry James/H.G. Wells Affair", *Extrapolation* vol 33, No 4, Winter 1992

ALLEN, Virginia, "The Ethos of English Departments: Henry James and H.G. Wells, Continued", *Extrapolation* vol 34, No 4, Winter 1993

AMIS, Kingsley, *New Maps of Hell*, Gollancz, 1961

ARMITT, Lucie (ed), *Where No Man has Gone Before*, Routledge, 1991

BUTLER, Marilyn, *Romantics, Rebels & Reactionaries: English Literature and its Background 1760-1830*, Oxford, 1981

CLUTE, John and Peter Nicholls (eds), *The Encyclopedia of Science Fiction*, Orbit, 1993

CONNOLLY, John, "A Progressive End: Arthur C. Clarke and Teilhard de Chardin", *Foundation 61*, Summer 1994

CORNWELL, Neil, *The Literary Fantastic: From Gothic to Postmodernism*, Harvester Wheatsheaf, 1990

DRABBLE, Margaret and Jenny Stringer (eds), *The Concise Oxford Companion to English Literature*, Oxford, 1990

FISHER IV, Benjamin Franklin, *The Gothic's Gothic: Study Aids to the Tradition of the Tale of Terror*, Garland, 1988

GREENLAND, Colin, *The Entropy Exhibition*, Routledge & Kegan Paul, 1983

HASSLER, Donald M., "Arthur Machen and Genre: Filial and Fannish Alternatives", *Extrapolation* vol 33, No 2, Summer 1992

KROEBER, Karl, *Romantic Fantasy and Science Fiction*, Yale, 1988

KUMAR, Krishan, *Utopia & Anti-Utopia in Modern Times*, Blackwell, 1987

LACY, Norris J. (ed), *The New Arthurian Encyclopedia*, St James Press, 1991

LEFANU, Sarah, *In the Chinks of the World Machine*, The Women's Press, 1988

LEWIS, C.S., *Of Other Worlds*, Geoffrey Bles, 1966

LOVECRAFT, Howard Phillips, *Supernatural Horror in Literature*, Dover, 1973

MANLOVE, C.N., *Modern Fantasy: Five Studies*, Cambridge, 1975

MOORCOCK, Michael, *Wizardry and Wild Romance*, Gollancz, 1987

PRIEST, Christopher, "British Science Fiction", *Science Fiction: A Critical Guide* (ed. Patrick Parrinder), Longman, 1979

PRINGLE, David, *Modern Fantasy: The Hundred Best Novels*, Grafton, 1988

PRINGLE, David, *The Ultimate Guide to Science Fiction*, Grafton, 1990

ROBINSON, Roger, "Early British SF Magazines", *Mexicon III Programme Book*, 1989

RUDDICK, Nicholas, *British Science Fiction: A Chronology, 1478-1990*, Greenwood Press, 1992

RUDDICK, Nicholas, *Ultimate Island: On the Nature of British Science Fiction*, Greenwood Press, 1993

STABLEFORD, Brian, *Scientific Romance in Britain 1890-1950*, Fourth Estate, 1985

SUVIN, Darko, *Metamorphoses of Science Fiction*, Yale University Press, 1980

TODOROV, Tzvetan, *The Fantastic: A Structural Approach to a Literary Genre*, Case Western Reserve, 1973

WATSON, Noelle and Paul E. Schellinger (eds), *Twentieth Century Science Fiction Writers: Third Edition*, St James Press, 1991

WILLIAMS, Gwyn A., *Excalibur: The Search for Arthur*, BBC, 1995

A Chronology

of British Fantasy and Science Fiction

A chronological listing of all the stories and novels referred to in the essay

1898	*The Rose of Judah* George Griffith
	The Sleeper Wakes H.G. Wells
	The Turn of the Screw Henry James
	The War of the Worlds H.G. Wells
	The Yellow Danger M.P. Shiel
1901	*The First Men in the Moon* H.G. Wells
	The Lord of the Sea M.P. Shiel
	The Purple Cloud M.P. Shiel
1902	*Five Children and It* E. Nesbit
	Just So Stories Rudyard Kipling
1903	"The Land Ironclads" H.G. Wells
1904	*Ghost Stories of an Antiquary* M.R. James
	"The Mezzotint" M.R. James
	The Napoleon of Notting Hill G.K. Chesterton
	"Oh Whistle and I'll Come to Thee, My Lad" M.R. James
1905	*A Modern Utopia* H.G. Wells
	The Yellow Wave M.P. Shiel
1906	*In the Days of the Comet* H.G. Wells
	Puck of Pook's Hill Rudyard Kipling
1907	"If Napoleon had Won the Battle of Waterloo" G.M. Trevelyan
	Lord of the World R.H. Benson
	"The Willows" Algernon Blackwood
1908	*The House on the Borderland* William Hope Hodgson
	The War in the Air H.G. Wells
	The Wind in the Willows Kenneth Grahame
1909	"The Machine Stops" E.M. Forster
	With the Night Mail Rudyard Kipling
1910	*Rewards and Fairies* Rudyard Kipling
1911	*An Exchange of Souls* Barry Pain
	The Centaur Algernon Blackwood
	More Ghost Stories of an Antiquary M.R. James
1912	*The Lost World* Arthur Conan Doyle
	The Nightland William Hope Hodgson
1913	*The Poison Belt* Arthur Conan Doyle
	When William Came H.H. Munro ("Saki")
	The Yellow Peril M.P. Shiel
1914	"The Bowmen" Arthur Machen
	The World Set Free H.G. Wells
1915	*The Bowmen and Other Legends of the War* Arthur Machen
	"The Great Return" Arthur Machen
1918-22	*Decline of the West* Oswald Spengler
1920	*The People of the Ruins* Edward Shanks
	A Voyage to Arcturus David Lindsay
1921	*The Bright Messenger* Algernon Blackwood
	"The Grisly Folk" H.G. Wells
1922	*The Worm Ouroboros* E.R. Eddison
1923	*The Clockwork Man* E.V. Odle
	Essays of a Biologist Julian Huxley
	Men Like Gods H.G. Wells
	"Seaton's Aunt" Walter de la Mare
	Uncanny Stories May Sinclair
1924	*Daedalus: or, Science and the Future*

	J.B.S. Haldane
	The King of Elfland's Daughter Lord Dunsany
1925	*Icarus: or, the Future of Science* Bertrand Russell
	Sir Gawain and the Green Knight J.R.R. Tolkien & E.V. Gordon
1927	*Deluge* S. Fowler Wright
	An Experiment with Time J.W. Dunne
	The Land of Mist Arthur Conan Doyle
	The Maracot Deep Arthur Conan Doyle
1928	*Great Short Stories of Detection, Mysery and Horror* ed. Dorothy L. Sayers
	Lest Ye Die Cicely Hamilton (revised version of *Theodore Savage* (1922))
1929	"When the World Screamed" Arthur Conan Doyle
	The World Below S. Fowler Wright (*The Amphibians* (1925) plus sequel)
	The World, the Flesh and the Devil J.D. Bernal
1930	*Last and First Men* Olaf Stapledon
	The Seventh Bowl Neil Bell ("Miles")
1931	*Dawn* S. Fowler Wright
	Look to the Lady Margery Allingham
	Many Dimensions Charles Williams
1932	*Brave New World* Aldous Huxley
	Dangerous Corner J.B. Priestley
	A Glastonbury Romance John Cowper Powys
	If It Had Happened Otherwise ed. J.C. Squire
	Last Men in London Olaf Stapledon
	Three Go Back J. Leslie Mitchell
	Tomorrow's Yesterday John Gloag
	"Worlds of Barter" John Beynon Harris (John Wyndham)
1933	*The Shape of Things to Come* H.G. Wells
1934	*Earth Stopped* T.H. White
	Gay Hunter J. Leslie Mitchell
1935	*Gone to Ground* T.H. White
	Odd John Olaf Stapledon
1936	*Laughing Gas* P.G. Wodehouse
1937	*The Hobbit* J.R.R. Tolkien
	I Have Been Here Before J B Priestley
	Morwyn John Cowper Powys
	Star Maker Olaf Stapledon
	Swastika Night Katherine Burdekin
	Time and the Conways J.B. Priestley
1938	*Out of the Silent Planet* C.S. Lewis
1938?	"On Fairy Tales" J.R.R. Tolkien
1941	"The Demon Lover" Elizabeth Bowen
1942	*The Screwtape Letters* C.S. Lewis
1943	*Perelandra* C.S. Lewis
1944	*Sirius* Olaf Stapledon
1945	*All Hallows' Eve* Charles Williams
	An Inspector Calls J.B. Priestley
	That Hideous Strength C.S. Lewis

The Infernal Desire Machines of Doctor Hoffman Angela Carter
Magog Andrew Sinclair
The Sheep Look Up John Brunner
"Weinachtsabend" Keith Roberts

1973
The Cloud Walker Edmund Cooper
Crash J.G. Ballard
The Embedding Ian Watson
The Hollow Hills Mary Stewart
Red Shift Alan Garner
Rendezvous with Rama Arthur C. Clarke
The Time of the Crack Emma Tennant

1974
"Ash, Ash" Robert Holdstock
The Chalk Giants Keith Roberts
Concrete Island J.G. Ballard
The Dream Millenium James White
Inverted World Christopher Priest
The Twilight of Briareus Richard Cowper

1975
The Birthgrave Tanith Lee
"The Custodians" Richard Cowper
Grimus Salman Rushdie
The Jonah Kit Ian Watson
Lud Heat Iain Sinclair
Orbitsville Bob Shaw
"Running Down" M. John Harrison
"Settling the World" M. John Harrison
The Shockwave Rider John Brunner

1976
The Alteration Kingsley Amis
The Dark Side of the Sun Terry Pratchett
"The Diary of the Translator" Geoff Ryman
Eye Among the Blind Robert Holdstock
The Space Machine Christopher Priest
A Wreath of Stars Bob Shaw

1977
The Book of Merlyn T.H. White
The Condition of Muzak Michael Moorcock
A Dream of Wessex Christopher Priest
Earthwind Robert Holdstock
In Solitary Garry Kilworth
The Martian Inca Ian Watson
The Passion of New Eve Angela Carter

1978
Merlin Robert Nye
The Night of Kadar Garry Kilworth
The Road to Corlay Richard Cowper
SS-GB Len Deighton
1985 Anthony Burgess

1979
The Bloody Chamber Angela Carter
Darkness Visible William Golding
The Last Enchantment Mary Stewart
Shikasta Doris Lessing

1980
Capella's Golden Eyes Christopher Evans
"Earth and Stone" Robert Holdstock
The Gardens of Delight Ian Watson
The Marriage Between Zones Three, Four, and Five Doris Lessing
Midnight's Children Salman Rushdie
"Outside the Whale" Christopher Priest
"The Stains" Robert Aickman
A Storm of Wings M. John Harrison

The Travails of Jane Saint (rev. 1986) Josephine Saxton

1981
The Affirmation Christopher Priest
Byzantium Endures Michael Moorcock
A Dream of Kinship Richard Cowper
"Egnaro" M. John Harrison
Lanark Alasdair Gray
"Mythago Wood" Robert Holdstock
Silver Metal Lover Tanith Lee
The Sirian Experiments Doris Lessing
The White Hotel D.M. Thomas

1982
In Viriconium M. John Harrison
The Making of the Representative for Planet 8 Doris Lessing
Mantissa John Fowles
Mother London Michael Moorcock
A Tapestry of Time Richard Cowper

1983
The Arabian Nightmare Robert Irwin
The Colour of Magic Terry Pratchett
The End of the World News Anthony Burgess
Golden Witchbreed Mary Gentle
The Sentimental Agents in the Volyen Empire Doris Lessing
"The Tithonian Factor" Richard Cowper

1984
Archer's Goon Diana Wynne Jones
The Book of the Night Rhoda Lerman
The Book of the River Ian Watson
Daybreak on a Different Mountain Colin Greenland
Divine Endurance Gwyneth Jones
The Empire of the Sun J.G. Ballard
The Glamour Christopher Priest
Legend David Gemmell
Mythago Wood Robert Holdstock
Nights at the Circus Angela Carter
"The Unconquered Country" Geoff Ryman
Viriconium Nights M. John Harrison
The Wasp Factory Iain Banks
1982, Janine Alasdair Gray

1985
The Book of Being Ian Watson
The Book of the Stars Ian Watson
Fire and Hemlock Diana Wynne Jones
Hawksmoor Peter Ackroyd
In Limbo Christopher Evans
The King Beyond the Gate David Gemmell
Kiteworld Keith Roberts
A Maggot John Fowles
"O Happy Day" Geoff Ryman
The Planet Dweller Jane Palmer
"Richenda" Keith Roberts
Tree Messiah Garry Kilworth
The Warrior Who Carried Life Geoff Ryman
"A Young Man's Journey to Viriconium" M. John Harrison

1986
Escape Plans Gwyneth Jones
Kaeti and Company Keith Roberts

51

The Limits of Vision Robert Irwin
O-Zone Paul Theroux
Queen of the States Josephine Saxton
The Rugged Astronauts Bob Shaw
Staring at the Sun Julian Barnes
The Unconquered Country Geoff Ryman
The Watcher Jane Palmer
Waylander David Gemmell
Witchwater Country Garry Kilworth
1987 Ancient Light Mary Gentle
The Child in Time Ian McEwan
Consider Phlebas Iain M. Banks
The Day of Creation J.G. Ballard
Dirk Gently's Holistic Detective Agency
Douglas Adams
Earthdoom! John Grant & David Langford
Einstein's Monsters Martin Amis
The Enchantments of Flesh and Spirit Storm
Constantine
Grainne Keith Roberts
"Hogfoot Right and Bird Hands"
Garry Kilworth
The Incomer Margaret Elphinstone
"Love Sickness" Geoff Ryman
The Power Ian Watson
A Tale of Time City Diana Wynne Jones
Valley of Lights Steve Gallagher
White Chappell, Scarlet Tracings
Iain Sinclair
1988 Abandonati Garry Kilworth
The Bewitchments of Love and Hate
Storm Constantine
The Child Garden Geof Ryman
Cloudrock Garry Kilworth
Desolation Road Ian McDonald
Empire Dreams Ian McDonald
Empire of Fear Brian Stableford
Forgotten Life Brian Aldiss
Kairos Gwyneth Jones
King Ludd Andrew Sinclair
Lavondyss Robert Holdstock
The Long Dark Tea-Time of the Soul
Douglas Adams
Player of Games Iain M. Banks
The Sykaos Papers E.P. Thompson
When the Tripods Came John Christopher
Wyrd Sisters Terry Pratchett
1989 Climbers M. John Harrison
The Fulfilments of Fate and Desire
Storm Constantine
Hunter's Moon Garry Kilworth
Jane Saint and the Backlash
Josephine Saxton
The Middle Kingdom David Wingrove
Pyramids Terry Pratchett
A Sparrow's Flight Margaret Elphinstone
White Nun's Telling Fay Sampson
Wise Woman's Telling Fay Sampson

1990 Black Smith's Telling Fay Sampson
Lion of Macedon David Gemmell
Quest for Lost Heroes David Gemmell
The Quiet Woman Christopher Priest
Rats and Gargoyles Mary Gentle
"Stalin's Teardrops" Ian Watson
Take Back Plenty Colin Greenland
The Time Lapsed Man Eric Brown
1991 Albion John Grant
The Architecture of Desire Mary Gentle
The Bone Forest Robert Holdstock
Correspondence Sue Thomas
Dark Prince David Gemmell
Eternal Light Paul J. McAuley
Expatria Keith Brooke
Hermetech Storm Constantine·
The Kindness of Women J.G. Ballard
King of Morning, Queen of Day
Ian McDonald
Mortal Mask Stephen Marley
Raft Stephen Baxter
Sexual Chemistry Brian Stableford
Taliesin's Telling Fay Sampson
Time's Arrow Martin Amis
White Queen Gwyneth Jones
1992 Anno Dracula Kim Newman
The Children of Men P.D. James
Chimeras Christopher Evans
The Course of the Heart M. John Harrison
Dark Sister Graham Joyce
Expatria Incorporated Keith Brooke
Fatherland Robert Harris
Hearts, Hands and Voices Ian McDonald
Herself Fay Sampson
Hot Head Simon Ings
Kaeti on Tour Keith Roberts
Lost Futures Lisa Tuttle
Memories of the Body Lisa Tuttle
Meridian Days Eric Brown
Poor Things Alasdair Gray
Shadow Sisters Stephen Marley
Was... Geoff Ryman
The World John Grant
1993 Against a Dark Background Iain M. Banks
Angel Garry Kilworth
Dancing on the Volcano Anne Gay
Flowerdust Gwyneth Jones
Harm's Way Colin Greenland
Here Comes the Sun Tom Holt
The Hollowing Robert Holdstock
House of Lost Dreams Graham Joyce
Lucky's Harvest Ian Watson
Mindstar Rising Peter F. Hamilton
Red Dust Paul J. McAuley
Sign for the Sacred Storm Constantine
Vurt Jeff Noon
1994 Aztec Century Christopher Evans
City of the Iron Fish Simon Ings

Engineman Eric Brown
The Fallen Moon Ian Watson
Faust Among Equals Tom Holt
Feersum Endjinn Iain M. Banks
Flux Stephen Baxter
A History Maker Alasdair Gray
Interesting Times Terry Pratchett
Left to her Own Devices Mary Gentle
North Wind Gwyneth Jones
Only Forward Michael Marshall Smith
Pasquale's Angel Paul J. McAuley
Radon Daughters Iain Sinclair

1995   *Blood Crazy* Simon Clark
Damned and Fancy John Brosnan
The Double Tongue William Golding
Exquisite Corpse Robert Irwin
Hotwire Simon Ings
Legacies Alison Sinclair
The Most Amazing Man Who Ever Lived Robert Rankin
Moths to a Flame Sarah Ash
The Prestige Christopher Priest
Seasons of Plenty Colin Greenland
The Time Ships Stephen Baxter
To Bathe in Lightning Anne Gay
Vivia Tanith Lee

A Checklist
of Contemporary British Fantasy and Science Fiction Authors

This checklist is not meant to be exhaustive. It is meant to provide an indication of the number and variety of British writers currently active in science fiction, fantasy, horror and related fields. Some are new writers whose first book is just appearing, others are household names approaching the ends of their careers. All testify to the health and the diversity of fantastic writing in this country.

Key:

f: fantasy   sf: science fiction
h: horror   ms: mainstream
c: children's

hg: Hugo Award
nb: Nebula Award
acc: Arthur C Clarke Award
bsfa: BSFA Award
jwc: John W Campbell
        Memorial Award
ifa: International Fantasy Award
pkd: Philip K Dick Award
wfa: World Fantasy Award

nv: novel   na: novella
nt: novelette   ss: short story
co: collection   nf: non-fiction

mrb: most recent book

Douglas ADAMS – sf
Awards:
    The Hitch-Hiker's Guide to the
Galaxy: bsfa-meda (3 times)
MRB: Mostly Harmless

Joan AIKEN – c/f/h
MRB: Cold Shoulder Road

Gill ALDERMAN – sf
MRB: An Unknown Paradise

Brian ALDISS – sf/ms
Awards:
    Hothouse: hg-nt
The Saliva Tree: nb-nv
The Moment of Eclipse: bsfa-c
Billion Year Spree: bsfa-nf
Trillion Year Spree: hg-nf
Helliconia Spring: bsfa/jwc-nv
Helliconia Winter: bsfa-nv
MRB: The Secret of this Book

Martin AMIS – ms
NW: Time's Arrow (1991)

Brian APPLEYARD – ms
MRB: The First Church of the New
Millenium

Sarah ASH – f
MRB: Moths to a Flame

Hilary BAILEY – ms/sf
MRB: Frankenstein's Bride

J.G. BALLARD – sf/ms
Awards:
    The Unlimited Dream
Company: bsfa-nv
MRB: Rushing to Paradise

Iain M. BANKS – sf/ms
Awards: Feersum Endjinn:
bsfa-nv/mrb

Clive BARKER – h/f
MRB: Everville

Stephen BAXTER – sf
MRB: The Time Ships

Barrington J. BAYLEY – sf
MRB: The Rod of Light

Chris BEEBEE – sf
MRB: The Hub

Peter BEERE – c/sf
MRB: Priests of Darkness

James BIBBY – f
MRB: Ronan the Barbarian

Chris BOYCE – sf
MRB: Brainfix

Chaz BRENCHLEY – h
MRB: Dead of Light

Keith BROOKE – sf
MRB: Expatria Incorporated

Christine BROOKE-ROSE –
ms/sf
MRB: Texterminations

John BROSNAN – sf
MRB: *Damned and Fancy*

Eric BROWN – sf
MRB: *Engineman*

John BRUNNER – sf
Awards:
   Stand on Zanzibar: bsfa/hg-nv
   The Jagged Orbit: bsfa-nv
MRB: *Children of the Thunder*

Mark BURNELL – h
MRB: *Glittering Savages*

A.S. BYATT – ms
MRB: *Angels and Insects*

Richard CALDER – sf
MRB: *Dead Boys*

David CALLINAN – sf
MRB: *Fortress Manhattan*

Ramsey CAMPBELL – h
MRB: *The One Safe Place*

Ronald
CAMPBELL-BUTLER – sf
MRB: *Fadar*

Mark CHADBOURN – h
MRB: *The Eternal*

Simon CLARK – sf
MRB: *Blood Crazy*

Arthur C. CLARKE – sf
Awards:
   The Star: hg-ss
   A Meeting with Medusa:
nb-na
   The Exploration of Space:
ifa-nf
   Rendezvous with Rama:
bsfa/hg/nb/jwc-nv
   Fountains of Paradise:
hg/nb-nv
MRB: *The Hammer of God*

D.G. COMPTON
MRB: *Justice City*

Storm CONSTANTINE – sf
MRB: *Stalking Tender Prey*

Louise COOPER – f
MRB: *Moonset*

Mary CORRAN – f
MRB: *Fate*

Richard COWPER – sf
MRB: *Shades of Darkness*

Peter DICKINSON – c
MRB: *Skeleton in Waiting*

Graham EDWARDS – f
MRB: *Dragon Charm*

Margaret ELPHINSTONE –
sf
MRB: *An Apple from a Tree*

Christopher EVANS – sf
Award:
   Aztec Century: bsfa-nv
MRB: *Mortal Remains*

Neil FERGUSON – sf/ms
MRB: *Double Helix Fall*

Christopher FOWLER – h
MRB: *Flesh Wounds*

John FOWLES – ms
MRB: *A Maggot*

Richard FRANCIS – sf
MRB: *Swansong*

Neil GAIMAN – f
MRB: *Sandman Anthology*

Ellen GALFORD – sf
MRB: *The Dyke and the Dybbuk*

Stephen GALLAGHER – h
MRB: *Red Red Robin*

David GARNETT – sf
MRB: *Stargonauts*

Anne GAY – sf
MRB: *To Bathe in Lightning*

David GEMMELL – f
MRB: *Hawk Eternal*

Mary GENTLE – sf
MRB: *Left to His Own Devices*

John GRANT – sf/f
MRB: *The World*

Alastair GRAY – ms
MRB: *A History Maker*

Simon R. GREEN – sf
MRB: *Hellworld*

Colin GREENLAND – sf
Awards:
   Take Back Plenty: acc/bsfa-nv
MRB: *Seasons of Plenty*

John GRIBBIN – sf
MRB: *The Ragnarok Alternative*
(with D.G. Compton)

Peter F. HAMILTON – sf
MRB: *The Reality Dysfunction*

W.A. HARBINSON – sf
MRB: *Millenium*

Robert HARRIS – ms
MRB: *Fatherland*

Steve HARRIS – h
MRB: *Black Rock*

M. John HARRISON – f
MRB: *Course of the Heart*

Gary HAYNES – h
MRB: *Carrion*

James HERBERT – h
MRB: *The Ghosts of Sleath*

Russell HOBAN – ms
Award:
  Riddley Walker: jwc-nv
MRB: *The Medusa Frequency*

Robert HOLDSTOCK – sf/f
Awards:
  Mythago Wood: bsfa-ss
  Mythago Wood: bsfa/wfa-nv
  Lavondyss: bsfa-nv
MRB: *Ancient Echoes*

Tom HOLLAND – ms
MRB: *The Vampyre*

Tom HOLT – f
MRB: *Djinn Rummy*

William HORWOOD – f
MRB: *Toad Triumphant*

Fred HOYLE – sf
MRB: *Comet Halley*

Shaun HUTSON – h
MRB: *Lucy's Child*

Simon INGS – sf
MRB: *Hotwire*

Robert IRWIN – ms
MRB: *Exquisite Corpse*

Brian JACQUES – f
MRB: *The Outcast of Redwall*

P.D. JAMES – ms
NW: *The Children of Men* (1992)

Peter JAMES – h
MRB: *Alchemist*

Phil JANES – sf
MRB: *I, Arnold*

Mike JEFFERIES – f
MRB: *The Knights of Cawdor*

Diana Wynne JONES – c/f
MRB: *A Sudden Wild Magic*

Gwyneth JONES – sf
MRB: *North Wind*

Jenny JONES – f
MRB: *The Blue Manor*

Mark JONES – h
MRB: *Black Lightning*

Graham JOYCE – f/h
MRB: *Requiem*

Paul KEARNEY – f
MRB: *Hawkwood's Voyage*

Garry KILWORTH – sf
MRB: *House of Tribes*

Joel LANE – h/f
MRB: *The Earth Wire*

David LANGFORD – sf
Award:
  Cube Root: bsfa-ss
MRB: *Earthdoom!* (with John
Grant)

Stephen LAWS – h
MRB: *Daemonic*

Tanith LEE – sf/f
MRB: *Vivia*

Anna LIVIA – sf
MRB: *Minimax*

Simon LOUVISH – ms
MRB: *What's Up God?*

Brian LUMLEY – h
MRB: *The Second Wish*

Paul McAULEY – sf
Award:
  400 Billion Stars: pkd-nv
MRB: *Fairyland*

Ian McDONALD – sf
Award:
  *King of Morning, Queen of
Day*: pkd-nv
MRB: *Chaga*

Ian McEWAN – ms
NW: *The Child in Time* (1987)

Ken MacLEOD – sf
MRB: *The Star Fraction*

Simon MAGINN – h
MRB: *Virgins and Martyrs*

Stephen MARLEY – f
MRB: *Shadow Sisters*

Graham Dunstan MARTIN –
sf
MRB: *Half a Glass of Moonshine*

Anita MASON – ms
NW: *The War Against Chaos*
(1988)

Naomi MITCHISON – ms/sf
NW: *Memoirs of a Spacewoman*
(1962)

Michael MOORCOCK – sf/f
Awards:
  Behold the Man: nb-na
  The Condition of Muzak:
guardian fiction prize-nv
  Gloriana: jwc-nv
MRB: *Blood*

Grant NAYLOR – sf
MRB: *Red Dwarf: The Last
Human*

Kim NEWMAN – sf/h
Award:
  The Original Dr Shade: bsfa-ss
MRB: *Famous Monsters*

Jeff NOON – sf
Award:
  Vurt: acc-nv
MRB: *Pollen*

Ben OKRI – ms
Award:
  The Famished Road:
booker-nv
MRB: *Astonishing the Gods*

Jane PALMER – sf
MRB: *Moving Moosevan*

Tim PARKS – ms
MRB: *Mimi's Ghost*

Amanda PRANTERA – ms/f
MRB: *The Kingdom of Fanes*

Terry PRATCHETT – f
Award:
   Pyramids: bsfa-nv
MRB: *Maskerade*

Christopher PRIEST – sf
Awards:
   Inverted World: bsfa-nv
   Palely Loitering: bsfa-ss
MRB: *The Prestige*

John PRITCHARD – h
MRB: *Angels of Mourning*

Robert RANKIN – sf
MRB: *The Garden of Unearthly Delights*

Keith ROBERTS – sf
Awards:
   Kitemaster: bsfa-ss
   Kaeti and the Hangman: bsfa-ss
   Grainne: bsfa-nv
MRB: *Kaeti on Tour*

Michael Scott ROHAN – f
MRB: *The Lord of Middle Air*

Nicholas ROYLE – h
MRB: *Counterparts*

William Moy RUSSELL – sf
MRB: *The Barber of Aldebaran*

Geoff RYMAN – sf/f
Awards:
   The Unconquered Country: bsfa/wfa-ss
   The Child Garden: acc/jwc-nv
MRB: *Was...*

Fay SAMPSON – f
MRB: *Star Dancer*

Josephine SAXTON – sf
MRB: *Jane Saint and the Backlash*

Michael SCOTT – f/h
MRB: *The Hallows*

Bob SHAW – sf
Award:
   Orbitsville: bsfa-nv
   the Ragged Astronauts: bsfa-nv
   Dark Night in Toyland: bsfa-ss
MRB: *Dark Night inToyland*

Alison SINCLAIR – sf
MRB: *Legacies*

Ian SINCLAIR – ms
MRB: *Radon Daughters*

Michael Marshall SMITH – sf
MRB: *Only Forward*

Brian STABLEFORD – sf
MRB: *Serpent's Blood*

Sue THOMAS – ms
MRB: *Water*

Patrick TILLEY – sf
MRB: *Star Wartz*

Philip TREWINNARD – h
MRB: *The Burning*

Lisa TUTTLE – sf/h
Awards:
   J.W. Campbell best new writer
   The Bone Flute: nb-ss (refused)
   In Translation: bsfa-ss
MRB: *Lost Futures*

Steve WALKER – sf
MRB: *21st Century Blues*

Freda WARRINGTON – f
MRB: *The Dark Blood of Poppies*

Ian WATSON – sf
Awards:
   The Jonah Kit: bsfa-nv
MRB: *The Fallen Moon*

Jane WELCH – f
MRB: *The Runes of War*

Angus WELLS – f
MRB: *Lords of the Sky*

John WHITBOURN – sf
MRB: *To Build Jerusalem*

David WINGROVE – sf
MRB: *Days of Bitter Strength*

Jonathan WYLIE – f
MRB: *Other Lands*

Index

What's happening
in science fiction today ...

Discover science fiction and you discover worlds beyond number. The British Science Fiction Association is your guide to these worlds. In reviews and interviews, articles and commentaries, we provide a constant source of information on what is happening in science fiction, as it happens. *Vector* brings you a lively and often controversial overview of sf by some of today's brightest stars. *Matrix* keeps you right up to date with all the latest news. *Focus* is the magazine for writers, with market news and professional tips. All for just £18 a year.

All it takes is a little imagination!